ETF
INVESTING
—— *for* ——
BEGINNERS

A STEP-BY-STEP GUIDE TO
BUILDING PASSIVE INCOME AND
LIFELONG WEALTH WITH LOW-RISK,
HIGH-REWARD STRATEGIES +
THE 7 BEST ETFs TO BUY TODAY

FREEMAN PUBLICATIONS

Want to learn more?

We regularly post videos on our YouTube channel—covering strategies, deep dives, and insights to help you go even further on your financial journey.

Whether you are just getting started or looking to sharpen your skills, you will find something valuable there.

To explore more, scan the QR code below or visit:

freemanpublications.com/youtube

TABLE OF CONTENTS

HOW TO GET THE MOST OUT OF THIS BOOK

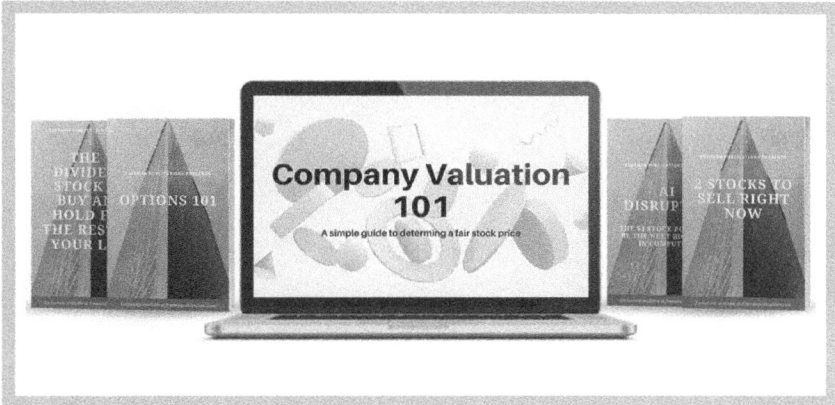

To help you along your investing journey, we've created a free bonus companion course that includes spreadsheets, bonus video content, and additional resources that will help you get the best possible results.

Including a video deep dive on my #1 crypto coin for 2024

This is the only new coin I believe can reach a $100 billion market cap in the next bull run. So to access this content free of charge, just to the link below or scan the QR code with your cell phone

https://freemanpublications.com/bonus

INTRODUCTION:
WHY THIS BOOK EXISTS

This book exists because more and more people are seeking a straightforward, sustainable path to financial security and independence.

Today, many people find themselves in one of two situations:

Position A: You want to build wealth for retirement or other long-term goals, but you're unsure of how to choose reliable, cost-effective investments.

Position B: You already have some investments but feel confused about how to make the most of your portfolio without getting bogged down in the complexities of stock picking.

If either of these situations applies to you, then you're in the right place. The first part of this book will break down where your investment approach might need clarity, and we'll unpack why "boring" investments, like ETFs (Exchange Traded Funds), can be the most reliable path toward achieving your goals.

What you won't find here is a list of overly complex strategies or hindsight advice that implies you should have been doing X or Y years ago. Instead, I'm going to guide you through practical, easy-to-apply steps so you can start investing—or refine your approach—regardless of where you're starting.

Once you've gotten a handle on ETFs and why they work, we'll go deeper. You'll learn how to select the right ETFs, build a diversified portfolio, and even apply advanced strategies to maximize your returns with minimal effort.

But here's the best part: this book assumes you don't have a finance degree, nor do you need to spend countless hours tracking the market. I'll show you how to navigate ETF investing, all while keeping things manageable and understandable. And yes, we'll even touch on how you can use the "Options Wheel Strategy" to boost your portfolio income just using ETFs.

If nothing else, remember these three key takeaways:

1. ETFs offer reliable, low-cost exposure to the market without the unpredictability of individual stocks.

2. A steady, diversified approach to investing can achieve more than the latest investment fads or stock tips.

3. With thoughtful, regular adjustments, you can keep your investment portfolio on track while dedicating minimal time each month.

ETF investing has been an essential part of my journey and my clients' journeys. I've seen firsthand how powerful a simple, disciplined approach can be in helping people achieve financial freedom, no matter their starting point.

Throughout the book, we have many additional resources available to you. Some resources, such as colour images, are much easier to deliver digitally. So to access those just head on over to freemanpublications. com/bonus

To your wealth,

Oliver El-Gorr
Founder & CEO, Freeman Publications
London, England
November 2024

Chapter 1

THE RISE OF PASSIVE INVESTING AND ETFS: TRACING THE ORIGINS

"The index fund was at first ridiculed, then tolerated, then grudgingly accepted, then reluctantly endorsed, and fine 18ally copied en masse."
- John C. Bogle

About halfway through Ernest Hemingway's 1926 breakthrough novel *The Sun Also Rises*, a character named Bill, a friend of the novel's protagonist, asks his friend Mike, "How did you go bankrupt?" "Two ways," Mike replies, "Gradually, and then suddenly."

Hemingway is not known for writing about investing. But these two lines from his work perfectly describe the humble origins followed by an explosive growth of passive investing and ETFs. When passive investing was introduced in the 1970s by John Bogle's Vanguard Group, using only 3 employees, its Index Investment Trust (now called 'Vanguard 500 Index Fund') raised just $11 million. That was far short of the $150 million target the fund had set. Vanguard's founder Bogle was ridiculed. The banks managing the Initial Public Offering (IPO) advised him to pull the plug on the fund and return investors' money as the fund struggled to gain traction.

Bogle persisted, and time would prove him right.

Passive investing first grew gradually and then all of a sudden it was everywhere. Launched in 1976, the Vanguard S&P 500 Index Fund didn't reach the $1 billion mark until 1990. Today, it manages assets valued at over $1.2 **trillion**, making it the second-largest equity index fund after the Vanguard Total Stock Market Index Fund valued at $1.7 trillion.

Passive investing, which only targets to match the broader market return (such as the S&P index) rather than beat it, was once mocked as 'un-American' and a 'sure path to mediocrity'. Today, more money is invested in passive funds than actively managed ones. According to fund performance research firm LSEG Lipper, at the end of December 2023, global passive equity funds' net assets stood at a record $15.1 trillion compared to $14.3 trillion managed by active equity funds.

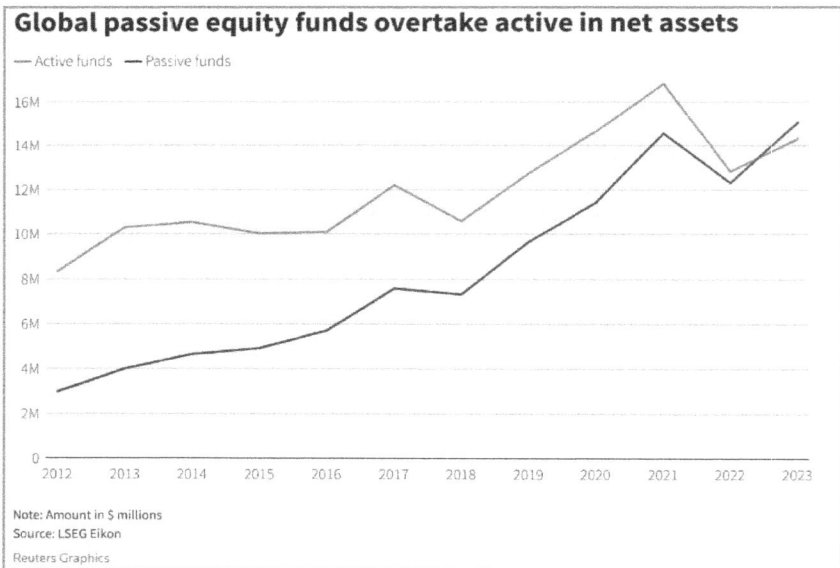

Global passive equity funds overtake active in net assets

Note: Amount in $ millions
Source: LSEG Eikon
Reuters Graphics

Figure 1: *Global passive equity funds overtake active in net assets (Source: www.reuters. com)*

Exchange Traded Funds (ETFs), the most recent innovation in passive investing, were introduced only in the 1990s. According to a PwC report, globally the total assets under management (AUM) of ETFs reached a new record of $11.5 trillion in 2023, achieving a remarkable

Compound Annual Growth Rate (CAGR) of 18.9% in the last 5 years (2018-23).

According to data from Statista Research, in the US alone ETFs have net assets of over $8 trillion (December 2023) clocking a nearly 5x growth in the last decade.

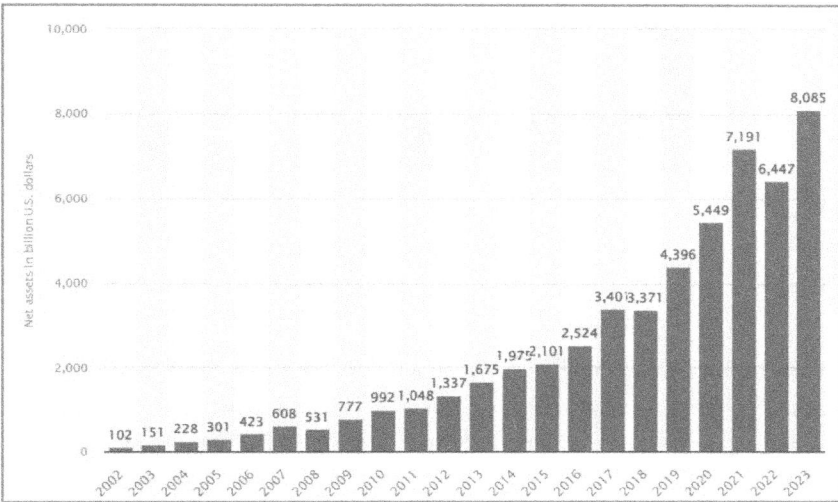

Figure 2: Explosive growth of ETFs in the US (Source: https://www.statista.com/)

In the same period, the share of actively managed funds has steadily declined at the cost of passive ones. In 2010, passively managed index funds accounted for just 19 percent of the total assets managed by U.S. investment companies, but by 2023, this share had risen to 48 percent.

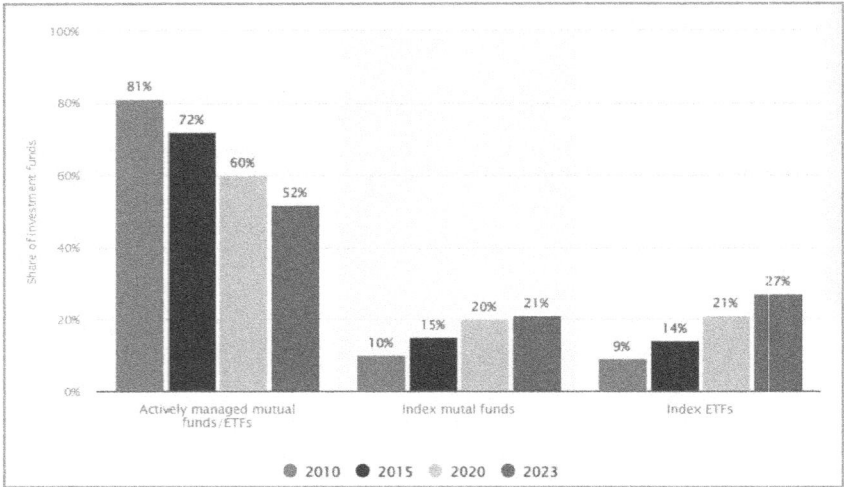

Figure 3: A steady decline in the share of active funds (Source: statista.com)

From being a subject of ridicule to a cornerstone of modern investing, passive investing has come a long way. But how did the passive investing movement get started and what were the triggers?

Let's trace the origins before we delve specifically into ETFs in the next chapters.

The first mutual fund, the crash and and call for regulations

Investors have always looked for creative ways to put their money to work while managing risks. One way to do so was to pool many investors' money and put it into diversified investment vehicles. Ones that were inaccessible or difficult to understand for an individual. The concept of pooled investment, which gave birth to modern mutual funds, was first introduced in Europe at the turn of the 19th century.

In the US the first closed-ended fund, the Boston Personal Property Trust, was launched in 1893. However, modern mutual fund was not introduced until 1924 when the first open-end fund, the Massachusetts Investors Trust (MIT - unrelated to the University with the same acronym). The fund still exists today, with an AUM of $6.9 billion

(June 2024). Open-ended funds brought in more transparency, higher liquidity, and professional management of investors' money compared to closed-ended ones which hardly disclosed their holdings and were heavily leveraged.

The booming stock market of the 1920s made these funds popular among investors who wanted a share of the swelling new wealth. Mutual funds were appealing because they allowed common investors to pool their money to invest in a diversified portfolio managed by professionals. This diversification helped reduce risk compared to investing in individual stocks, making it a better option for average investors. Between 1927 and 1929, the number of funds grew from 75 to 181; and the value of assets they managed from $600 million to over $2.7 billion.

The optimism was short-lived though.

The stock market crash in 1929 followed by the great depression wiped out most of these mushrooming investment companies. By 1932, Dow Jones was down by 80% from its 1929 peak and the MIT fund had lost 75% of its value. Closed-ended funds performed worse because of their highly leveraged positions. Soon, words like "investment trust" and "investment management" became dirty words to investors. They shied away from any type of managed funds until the economy started recovering.

The stock market rout of the 1930s led to the public demand for more regulation, transparency, and accountability. Some even called for a complete ban on investment companies. According to Barnie Winkelman, a Philadelphia attorney

> *"After careful consideration, the writer finds little justification for investment trusts of any kind...The entire plan of the investment trust is a snare for men of small means."*

Public outcry for more government intervention in the securities market led to two key pieces of legislation:

1. The Securities Act of 1933

2. The Investment Company Act of 1940.

These helped re-establishing public confidence in securities and fuel the next bout of growth in the mutual fund industry.

From the end of 1929 through 1940, mutual fund assets in the US grew more than 3x from $140 million to $450 million. What followed was a secular post-war growth in mutual funds investment, from $2 billion in value in 1950 to about $17 billion in 1960 coinciding with an astounding growth in the US economy. Hundreds of new funds were launched to serve new investors.

The efficient market, random walk, and the rise of indexing

While fund managers were having a great time in the 1950s and '60s, a couple of new investing philosophies emerged to challenge their unquestionable authority. For instance, the Efficient Market Hypothesis (EMH) introduced in the 1960s attacked a key assumption of the mutual funds industry that fund managers can actively select undervalued stocks and beat the market.

The theory, developed independently by American economists Paul Samuelson and Eugene Fama, showed that stock prices efficiently reflect all available information. This means there is no way to know which stock is 'overvalued' or 'undervalued' as the current price of a stock reflects all public information. So, why would investors pay the fund managers to do something that's theoretically impossible?

This was the first major attack on active fund management. The EMH directly challenged the idea that active fund managers could consistently beat the market by identifying undervalued or overvalued stocks. Then came another theory - the theory of the random walk, popularized by economist Burton Malkiel's book *A Random Walk Down Wall Street* (1973). The core theme of the book is that stock price movements are random and it's impossible to predict them. This means even the most sophisticated equity analyst has no edge in picking stocks and beating the market.

As these theories established that it's foolish to try to beat the market, a new investing idea emerged: If the market cannot be beaten, why not simply stick to market returns while avoiding excess management fees (mutual funds are expensive because of the way they are structured and they function. More on this in the next chapter)?

This led to a new era in investing - the era of index funds and passive investing.

Bogle's folly

New investing theories in the 1960s and '70s, established that investors may be better off "buying the market" rather than picking individual stocks. "Buying the market", also called indexing, is a passive investment strategy in which money is put in a fund replicating a broad index like the S&P 500. It needs no security analyst, no portfolio manager, and no sophisticated stock-picking formula. This means low costs in managing these funds.

Indexing democratizes investment. It's the friend of common investors, and, of course, the enemy of the active fund managers! Prof. Samuelson, one of the early proponents of passive investing and Bogle's mentor, said:

> *"...most portfolio managers should go out of business – take up plumbing, teach Greek, or help produce the annual GNP by serving as corporate executives."*

The first index mutual fund was born when John C. Bogle, the founder of the Vanguard Group, started the First Index Investment Trust. His vision was to make investment simple, easy, and cost-effective for common investors through a low-cost index fund. Of course, he was immediately laughed at by critics who called his index fund 'Bogle's folly'. They thought it was a stupid idea to settle for a just average market return.

However, Bogle had the last laugh.

Index funds had a slow growth in the 1970s due to a sluggish market and an economy stuck in stagflation. Starting with $11 million in 1976, index funds grew to only $511 million by 1985. However, an epic bull market starting in 1982 provided fresh air under the wings of passive funds. In the decade between 1985-95, they had an outrageous 100x growth to $55 billion.

The rise of ETFs: surpassing mutual funds in growth

By the 1990s, passive investing already cemented its position with more investors buying the idea and industry veterans cheering for it. In 1993 Warren Buffett, in a letter to shareholders, wrote

"By periodically investing in an index fund, for example, the know-nothing investor can actually outperform most investment professionals. Paradoxically, when 'dumb' money acknowledges its limitations, it ceases to be dumb."

While index mutual funds gained popularity among common investors, a key thing was lacking in them. They could not be traded in the exchanges. Investors could redeem their shares with the fund owner only at the end of a day's trading session. Computer-based investing platforms just came in. So, investors were looking for something that gives the benefits of indexing and the tradability of stocks.

This is precisely what exchange-traded funds (ETFs) do.

ETFs are simply an extension of index-based mutual funds. It's that ETFs are more tax-efficient, cost-effective, flexible, and liquid. ETFs can be traded in the stock exchanges just like stocks and other securities. Plus, they can be sold short and traded in the futures and options markets just as stocks are. So, ETFs combine the features of both index funds and individual stocks.

The SPDR S&P 500 ETF Trust (SPY), launched by State Street Global Advisors in 1993, was the first ETF to be listed in the US. Starting with just $6.53 million in AUM, SPY soared to more than $1 billion within 3 years. Over thirty years later, there are now more than 12,000 ETFs globally tracking specific industries, sectors, commodities, and geographies. And yet, SPY remains the largest and most traded ETF in the world with an AUM of over $553 billion (September 2024) and an average daily trading volume of $34 billion.

ETFs democratize investing by empowering millions of everyday investors to combine the power of indexing while enjoying the liquidity and flexibility of stocks. According to the Investment Company Institute, an estimated 15.2 million, or about 12 percent, of US households held ETFs in 2023.

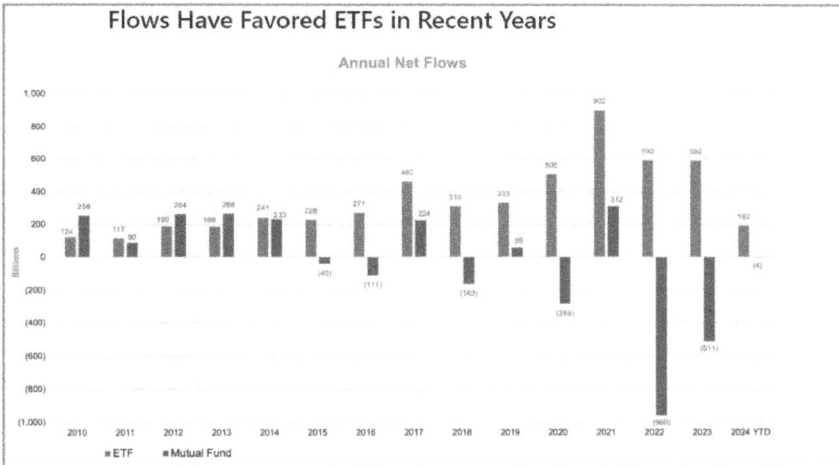

Figure 4: Annual net flows into ETFs and mutual funds (Source: americancentury.com)

In the US alone ETFs have attracted a net inflow of about a gigantic $2 trillion in the last 3 years. In comparison, mutual funds have posted net outflows for four of the past six years, including losses of almost $960 billion in 2022 and over $500 billion in 2023.

ETFs too happened gradually, and then suddenly!

Wrapping it up

You'll often hear the phrase, "Past performance is no guarantee of future results." While this is especially true for individual investments, the long-term success of index investing as a whole is undeniable. For instance, a typical investor in the S&P 500 can expect returns of 9-10% over 20 years, but missing just 10 of the best days in the market could cut those returns in half!

Trying to time the market has proved to be a losing strategy in the stock market. The simple strategy of staying invested in the long run with the broader market can have miraculous results for the average investor (read the story of how Warren Buffett challenged and won against a hedge fund manager, in the next chapter).

As you'll see, broad market ETFs and index funds are merely a representation of large corporations' earnings over a long period. To bet against that is to bet against the entire capitalist system!

Chapter 2

BORING IS GOOD

"Investing should be more like watching paint dry or watching grass grow. If you want excitement, take $800 and go to Las Vegas."
*- **Paul Samuelson**, American economist.*

Do stocks outperform Treasury bills?

B ack in 2016, Hendrik Bessembinder, a finance professor at Arizona State University, was searching for an answer to this seemingly simple question. Looking at soaring stocks in recent years, the conclusion may seem obvious to many. But, Bessembinder wanted to go beyond anecdotes and look for statistical evidence.

He started with a gigantic sample size of 25,362 stocks - including almost every publicly traded US company in the 90 years between 1926 and 2016. The study was extended in 2022 to 28,114 stocks to include newly listed firms. The prolific equity researcher found that the US stock market created a net cumulative wealth of over $55 trillion between 1926-2022, which is roughly 40% of the total wealth created in the US in that period. (Note: In a rough comparison, the total wealth in the US increased by about $135 trillion between 1929 and 2023).

The interesting part is that <u>half</u> of that $55 Trillion came from only 72 firms—less than 0.26% of the sample while one-tenth of the $55 trillion was attributed to just 3 stocks! Apple (4.86%), Microsoft (3.80%), and Exxon Mobil (2.21%).

That however wasn't the most startling discovery.

The <u>entire</u> $55.11 trillion of net wealth created in the US stock market between 1926 and 2022, came from just a minuscule 3.436% of all publicly traded stocks. This means, that over 96% of all US stocks traded during the last century resulted in a net wealth gain of ZERO.

And, the majority of stocks (58.6%) simply destroyed wealth, generating negative returns.

Table 2: Proportions of Total Net and Gross Wealth Creation Accounted for by Indicated Number of Firms						
	1926 to 2016		1926 to 2019		1926 to 2022	
Total Number Firms	25,362		26,150		28,114	
Net Shareholder Wealth Creation	$34.82 trillion		$47.39 trillion		$55.11 trillion	
Gross Shareholder Wealth Creation	$40.84 trillion		$54.25 trillion		$64.23 trillion	
Panel A: Net Wealth Creation						
	Number Firms	% of Firms	Number Firms	% of Firms	Number Firms	% of Firms
Fraction of Net Wealth Creation						
10%	5	0.020%	4	0.015%	3	0.011%
20%	14	0.055%	13	0.050%	11	0.039%
30%	29	0.114%	26	0.099%	23	0.082%
40%	53	0.209%	47	0.180%	42	0.149%
50%	90	0.355%	83	0.317%	72	0.256%
60%	148	0.584%	139	0.532%	120	0.427%
70%	235	0.927%	226	0.864%	196	0.697%
80%	375	1.479%	369	1.411%	317	1.128%
90%	621	2.449%	627	2.398%	528	1.878%
100%	1,094	4.314%	1,173	4.486%	966	3.436%
Panel B: Gross Wealth Creation						
	Number Firms	% of Firms	Number Firms	% of Firms	Number Firms	% of Firms
Fraction of Gross Wealth Creation						
10%	7	0.028%	5	0.019%	4	0.014%
20%	18	0.071%	16	0.061%	14	0.050%
30%	40	0.158%	34	0.130%	31	0.110%
40%	76	0.300%	66	0.252%	61	0.217%
50%	138	0.544%	121	0.463%	110	0.391%
60%	238	0.938%	212	0.811%	195	0.694%
70%	416	1.640%	372	1.423%	343	1.220%
80%	764	3.012%	688	2.631%	632	2.248%
90%	1,578	6.222%	1,464	5.598%	1,372	4.880%
100%	10,669	42.067%	11,020	42.141%	11,633	41.378%
Panel C: Firms With Negative Shareholder Wealth Creation						
Firms With Negative Wealth Creation	14,693	57.933%	15,130	57.859%	16,481	58.622%

Table 1: *Concentration of Stock Market Returns in the US (Source: papers.ssrn.com)*

In a separate global study, Bessembinder found that the top-performing 2.4% of firms account for all of the $US 75.7 trillion in net global stock market wealth creation from 1990 to December 2020.

The question then is how the US stock market as a whole generated an impressive compounded annual return of more than 10% (compared to 6% by long-term corporate bonds) in the last century, despite more than 9 out of 10 stocks having no contribution to said return.

The answer is that a select handful of powerhouse companies (called "superstocks") —such as Apple, Microsoft, Amazon, and most recently, Nvidia—have delivered exceptional returns that have more than compensated for the underperformance of the majority of stocks ever listed on exchanges.

Stock investing would be fun if one could spot those superstocks in the early days. But can we?

Needles in a stock picker's haystack: can you find the 3.5%?

Apple alone has generated about one-twentieth (4.86%) of the vast wealth created in the US stock market in the last century. But is there a proven way to pick such outstanding stocks in their early days? And, even if there were a secret method, how many investors would you find with the mettle of holding to Apple for 3 decades with multiple near-death experiences? According to NYSE estimates, the average investor today only holds individual stocks for 5.5 months, down from 8 years in the 1950s and 2 years in the 1990s.

Between 1992 and 1997, Apple's stock fell by 79.6% underperforming the S&P 500 by a staggering 771%. This means $1 invested in both Apple and the S&P 500 in 1992 would result in $0.23 and $2.23 respectively by the end of 1997.

In September 2000, the stock plummeted by 52% in a single day after the company slashed its earnings forecast. This wasn't the only large drawdown Apple suffered. In 2008, following the global financial crisis, Apple's stock closed the year down 56.9%!

Finding great stocks is challenging, but holding onto them is even harder. David Salem, Managing Director of Capital Allocation at Hedgeye Risk Management, said:

> *"There are no investment professionals in the world who bought Apple 30 years ago and held it continuously ever since -- except liars."*

Superstocks like Apple or Amazon have big payoffs in the long run. However, with around 60,000 publicly listed stocks worldwide, for every Apple or Amazon, there are thousands of losers like Pets.com, ValueAmerica, Enron, Blockbuster, Lehman Brothers, and eToys, leaving investors' money up in smoke.

> **The bottom line**: Only about 3.5% of all stocks create all the wealth in the stock market. Finding them is hard and staying invested in them is even harder. A more modest and realistic approach for the everyday investor is to "buy the market," betting that a few big winners—those that return 10 or even 100 times their value—will lift the overall portfolio and still provide a solid return.

What's interesting is that despite overwhelming evidence, even the best of Wall Street fall for the seduction of picking individual stocks.

But, do they succeed?

Warren Buffett's challenge

Imagine for a moment that you've got $10,000 to invest. There are 2 options in front of you: You could either pour that money into an S&P 500 index fund or a portfolio of hedge funds – the pinnacle of stock selection, managed by the industry's very best.

What's your pick?

Before you make up your mind, let's take a little trip back to 2008. Picture yourself making this very investment decision back then. And here's the twist - by the end of 2017, your $10,000 in the seemingly elite hedge fund portfolio would've grown to $13,630, a respectable 36.3% return. Not bad, right?

But hold onto your hat, because the supposedly "boring" index fund option would've turned your $10,000 into a whopping $22,580, boasting a 125.8% total return.

This wasn't, however, a hypothetical scenario.

Back in 2007, Warren Buffett proposed a bet with the leading investment experts of Wall Street. Buffett had a simple proposition: If someone invests in a low-cost index fund like the S&P 500 index fund and just sits tight, they would perform better than any expert-managed active fund in 10 years. He offered to wager $500,000 for the bet expecting a large number of professional fund managers would challenge him.

Surprisingly no one from the fund management community was ready to take the challenge!

Eventually, one hedge fund manager – Ted Seides, of Protege Partners – stepped forward. The bet was officially on - starting from January 1st, 2008. In response to Buffett's Vanguard S&P 500 Fund, Protege Partners chose five fund-of-funds. Each of these funds contained a variety of hedge funds including carefully chosen global stocks, managed by 5 investment managers and assisted by hundreds of investment experts.

When the final result was out on 31st December 2017, Buffett's index fund clocked a total return of 125.8% relative to the total return of 36.3% by the hedge funds. The S&P index fund provided an average annual growth rate of 8.5% while Protege's investment fetched merely 2.2% net of fees and charges.

The writing is clear: For most people, betting on the overall market is a much more effective strategy than picking individual stocks.

Active vs. Passive—the SPIVA Reports

For over 20 years, S&P Global has been publishing its renowned S&P Indices versus Active (SPIVA) report demonstrating the performance of passive funds vis-a-vis active ones. Its most recent SPIVA Scorecard shows that about 88% of all active large-cap funds in the US underperformed the S&P 500 index in the last 15 years.

SPIVA (S&P Indices Versus Active)

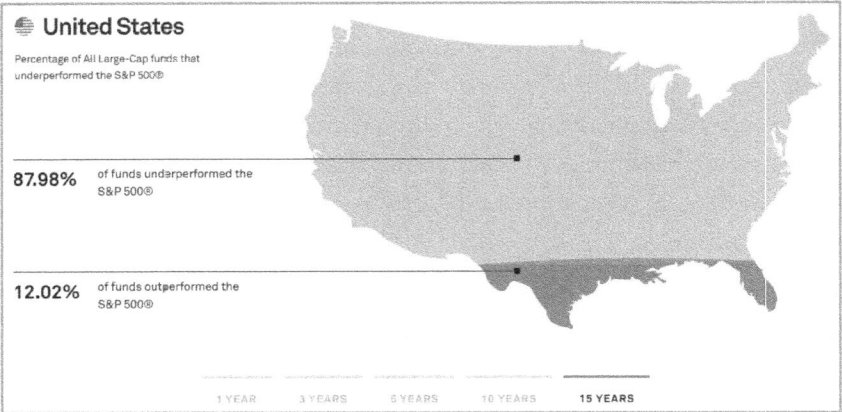

United States

Percentage of All Large-Cap funds that
underperformed the S&P 500®

87.98% of funds underperformed the
S&P 500®

12.02% of funds outperformed the
S&P 500®

1 YEAR   3 YEARS   5 YEARS   10 YEARS   **15 YEARS**

Figure 5: 88% of active large-cap funds underperforming the S&P 500 (Source: S&P Global)

If we take a shorter time horizon of five years, the underperformance rate of active funds slightly drops to 79%.

This means two things: 1. Passive beats active investing with an overwhelming majority, and 2. Passive investing tends to perform even better in the longer term.

Skill or luck?

So, if the case for passive investing is so strong, why does active investing still exist? The answer is that at times, especially in the short term, some active managers have managed to beat the market. It isn't uncommon for fund managers to outperform the market in a particular year. Some even did it for several years in a row. For instance, under the legendary investor Peter Lynch, the Fidelity Magellan Fund delivered a stunning 29.2% compounded annual return for 13 years between 1977 to 1990. This means a thousand dollars invested the day Lynch took over the fund would have been worth US$ 28,000 the day he quit.

That was double the S&P 500's performance over the same period.

But after Lynch, no fund manager at Magellan could repeat the same feat. In the last 10 years (as of June 2024), the Fidelity Magellan Fund, achieved an average annual return of 13.12% barely matching the 12.98% return by the S&P 500 in the same period.

When it comes to beating the market, it's difficult to separate individual miracles (and sometimes plain luck) from skills, which can be learned and passed on. Outperforming the market, however, is often a one-time wonder.

S&P Global studied the performance of 1,118 actively managed funds whose performance over the 12 months ending December 2019 put them in the top quartile in their respective categories. Out of these, only 2 funds remained in the top quartile in each of the four subsequent one-year periods ending December 2023. And only 2% of all large-cap equity funds remained in the top half over five years ending December 2023.

Exhibit 1: Only 2% of All Large-Cap Equity Funds Remained in the Top Half Over a Five-Year Period

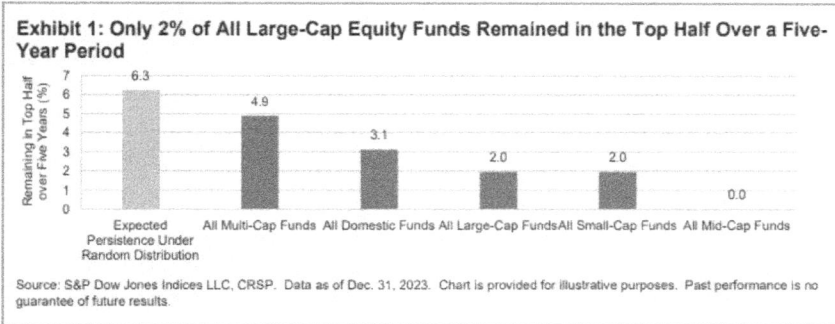

Source: S&P Dow Jones Indices LLC, CRSP. Data as of Dec. 31, 2023. Chart is provided for illustrative purposes. Past performance is no guarantee of future results.

Figure 6: Outperformance is inconsistent (Source: S&P Dow Jones Indices LLC, CRSP)

So, if even the best of fund managers struggle to consistently outperform the market, what chance do everyday investors have? Luckily, they have a sampler tool to participate in the broader market to build enormous wealth in the long term.

A game-changing innovation in passive investing

While buying the market is a simple and effective strategy for the average investor, you can't literally "buy the market" as a whole. The cost of buying every stock on the S&P 500 is prohibitively high (even if we ignore the hassle of managing 500 individual stocks). We need other ways.

One way to invest in the broader market is through an index fund. These are mutual funds that track a market index like the S&P 500. However, index mutual funds can't be traded like common stocks on exchanges. You can buy an index mutual only from a fund provider. Once purchased, your share can be redeemed at the end-of-day NAV (net asset value). Index funds are costlier because of the way they are designed and managed. Moreover, in most cases, you need to make a minimum investment of $500 to $3,000 to participate in an index mutual fund.

Now, imagine converting the S&P 500 or the FTSE 100 index into a single stock that can be traded just like other stocks throughout the trading session. This is precisely what ETFs do. Most popular ETFs are based on passive investing and they track an index (although there are actively managed ETFs as well).

ETFs offer the diversification benefits (your money is spread across all the stocks on an index) of index funds along with the tradability and flexibility of individual stocks. The flexibility of trading, however, is not the only feature that makes ETFs a great investing tool (frequent trading often leads to losses).

ETFs offer a host of other benefits:

◇ **No minimum investment**: In most cases, there is no minimum investment requirement to participate in ETFs (mutual funds generally require a minimum investment of $500 to $3,000).

◇ **Lower costs:** In general, ETFs involve much lower costs compared to index funds or active mutual funds. The expense ratio of an average ETF is around half of that of an average mutual fund (0.50% vs 1.01%). Plus, unlike mutual funds, ETFs don't involve marketing fees (called a 12b-1 fee) or sales loads (commission charged while buying or selling mutual fund shares).

◇ **Higher accessibility:** You can invest in ETFs, just like stocks, using a regular brokerage account.

◇ **Greater flexibility**: ETFs can be bought and held, shorted, and traded in the derivative market through futures and options.

◇ **Better transparency**: Most ETFs disclose their holdings daily while mutual funds typically make their holdings public once every quarter.

◇ **Tax advantages**: Since passive ETFs don't buy and sell their holdings frequently, they offer tax advantages compared to active mutual funds. We will discuss these tax advantages in more detail in later chapters.

ETFs are of different types depending on the underlying asset (stocks, bonds, commodities, or even crypto). The most common and sought-after ETFs are index ETFs (for example, SPDR S&P 500 or iShares Russell 2000). Think of an index ETF as a single stock, yet diversified across the entire market, that guarantees the broader market return. This book focuses mainly on index ETFs—the boring ones! They allow you to stay invested in the entire stock market for as little as $1. And, they allow a safe way for beginners to get started with stock investing.

How ETFs are created and redeemed

ETFs can be bought and sold on exchanges just like stocks. So when you buy a share of the SPDR S&P 500 using your brokerage account, you are essentially buying it from another investor who wants to sell it. But how are ETF shares introduced in the market for the first time and how are they redeemed?

This happens through a process called creation and redemption. The ETF sponsors (such as Blackrock, Vanguard, and State Street) don't introduce ETFs directly in the secondary market. This is done through Authorized Participants (APs) (which are typically large financial institutions like Goldman Sachs and JPMorgan Chase).

APs gather the underlying securities (for example, all 500 stocks in the S&P 500) of the fund in the right proportion and deliver these securities to the ETF sponsor. They in turn package these securities into ETF shares and deliver them to the APs, who introduce these newly created ETF shares to the secondary market, where they can be traded by investors on the exchange.

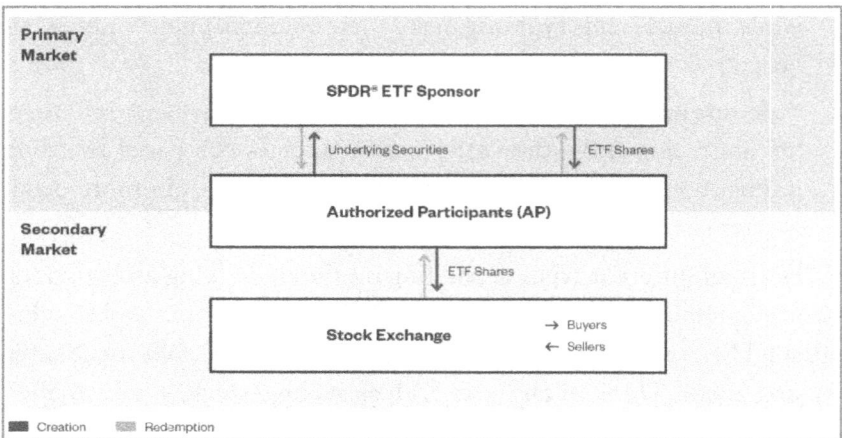

Figure 7: Creation and Redemption of ETFs (Source: www.ssga.com)

While redemption, this process is just reversed. APs collect large blocks of ETF shares, known as redemption units, from the secondary market and send them back to the ETF sponsor in exchange for the underlying securities.

This unique creation and redemption process ensures that the ETF's portfolio manager doesn't need to buy or sell individual securities, except for periodic rebalancing. This is how ETFs cut a significant amount of management costs.

Wrapping it up

Active investors often ridicule index funds and ETFs because they mechanically own every stock in a market benchmark. This often means holding overpriced stocks and riding them down rather than trying to buy and sell all the time (which they call 'timing the market'). However, it's these passive investment methods that don't sell Apple's stock when it drops by 50% because when it goes up, they get to go along for the full upswing.

Time and again, it has been proved that "time in the market" is better than "timing the market". ETFs are probably one of the most consistent and "boring" ways of making money in the long run. And, when it comes to long-term investing, the boring is good.

Chapter 3

THERE'S AN ETF FOR EVERYTHING

"Thousands of experts study overbought indicators, head-and-shoulder patterns, put-call ratios, the Fed's policy on money supply... and they can't predict markets with any useful consistency, any more than the gizzard squeezers could tell the Roman emperors when the Huns would attack."
- Peter Lynch.

It was October 19, 1987—a typical bright autumn morning in New York. The mood in the New York Stock Exchange (NYSE), however, was pretty somber. The Dow Jones index had crashed by an unprecedented 508 points (22.6%— the equivalent of the Dow falling <u>over 9,000 points</u> in a single session today) while the S&P 500 fell by over 20%. It was the biggest one-day market sell-off in US history. Globally, $1.7 trillion was wiped out in a single day.

This was the infamous 'Black Monday,' a day that would go down in history for its dramatic market collapse.

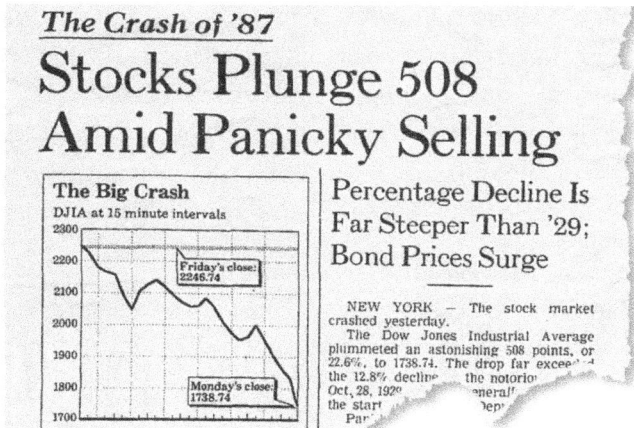

The Crash of '87

Stocks Plunge 508
Amid Panicky Selling

The Big Crash
DJIA at 15 minute intervals

**Percentage Decline Is
Far Steeper Than '29;
Bond Prices Surge**

NEW YORK — The stock market crashed yesterday.
The Dow Jones Industrial Average plummeted an astonishing 508 points, or 22.6%, to 1738.74. The drop far exceeded the 12.8% decline the notorio...

Figure 8: *The crash of 1987 - the black Monday (Source: WSJ.com)*

Several underlying factors—such as a stock market bubble, a larger-than-expected trade deficit in the US, and the depreciating dollar—contributed to the market's sharp decline that day. However, the three immediate reasons for Black Monday's market crash were computerized trading triggering stop losses, portfolio insurance[1], and panicked mutual funds dumping their holdings.

In the aftermath, market regulators were scurrying to find ways to prevent a similar crash. Among the solutions introduced were changes in the settlement cycles (of stocks, options, and futures) and circuit breakers (they automatically halt trading when the market or a specific stock declines by a certain percentage). However, another innovative investment instrument was created in response to Black Monday, specifically designed to address market volatility.

It was ETFs.

---

1 - (*Note: Because of the Portfolio insurance strategies, large institutional investors were designed to automatically take short future positions when stocks fell below a certain percentage. On Black Monday, as the market continued to decline, large investors sold short more S&P 500 futures contracts. This downward pressure in the futures market intensified selling in the stock market as well)*

Nathan Most, an American Stock Exchange executive, along with his team—including Steven Bloom—set out to analyze the 1987 crash. They found a new method for trading baskets of securities. After extensive trial and error and a challenging journey with the Securities and Exchange Commission (SEC), they finally launched the first ETF in the US, the SPDR S&P 500 Trust ETF (nicknamed "The Spider"), on January 22, 1993.

Born from the ashes of Black Monday, ETFs rose like the proverbial phoenix. The US alone has now (September 2024) more than 3,400 ETFs up from 2,113 in June 2020 and 1,376 in 2014.

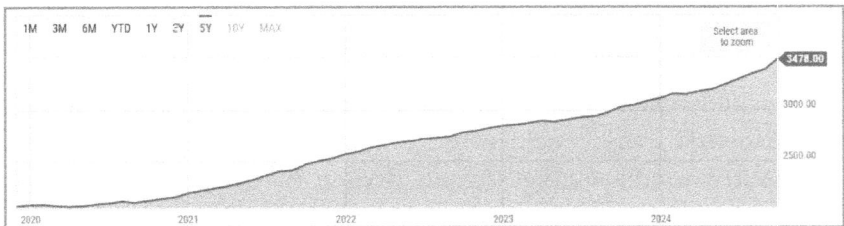

Figure 9: Growth in the number of ETFs in the US (Source: ycharts.com)

According to ETFGI, a London-based ETF research platform, by the end of August 2024, globally there were 12,677 ETFs from 774 providers listed on 81 exchanges in 63 countries. Together, they hold an AUM of over $13.99 trillion. 1,192 of these ETFs were launched in just 8 months between Jan-Aug 2024!

It's thanks to ETFs that retail investors can anchor a significant portion of their portfolios to the relative safety of blue-chip US stocks while still playing around with emerging market stocks or bonds or even new themes like AI and crypto.

There is now an ETF for everything. But which ones suit your needs?

Let's explore.

Major ETF Types

Most ETFs include a basket of assets traded on an exchange. These assets can be stocks, bonds, commodities, currencies, real estate, and alternative assets like cryptocurrencies. More than 93% of ETF assets in the USA are invested in index ETFs.

The most common ETFs are equity ETFs (79% of the entire US ETF market valuation, 6.39 trillion AUM), followed by bond ETFs (18.9%, 1.53 trillion AUM), and commodity ETFs (1.6%, 0.13 trillion AUM).

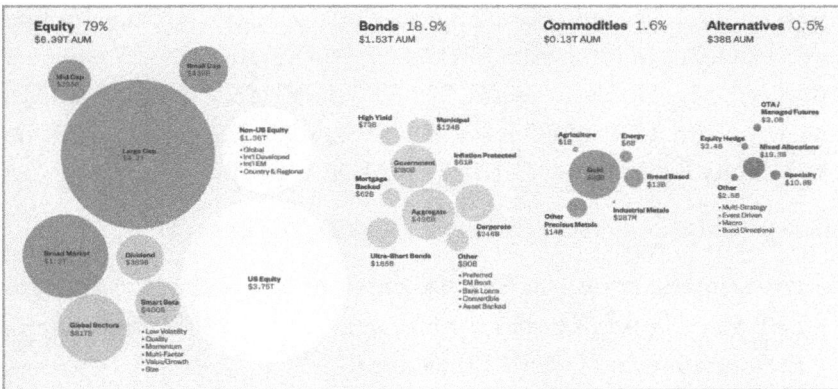

Figure 10: *Distribution of ETFs in the US (Source: www.ssga.com)*

These ETFs can be of different types based on factors like underlying assets (stocks. Bonds, or gold), geography (global ETFs, US ETFs, and emerging market ETFs), the index it tracks (S&P 500 or Nikkei 225 ETFs), market cap (large, medium, small-cap ETFs), investment theme (artificial intelligence or high-yield bonds), or sector (tech, energy or pharma).

You can invest in ETFs to gain exposure to an entire asset class (stocks, bonds, or real estate), the broader market (S&P 500), a very specific segment (US tech or Japanese manufacturing stocks), or a basket of securities based on a factor like a dividend yield (for example Vanguard International High Dividend Yield ETF (VYMI).

Let's now look at some of the major types of ETFs.

1. Equity ETFs

For an equity ETF, the underlying asset is stocks. Most equity ETFs track a broader market index like the S&P 500. More than half of the entire ETF AUM in the US is concentrated in large-cap stocks ($4.3 trillion).

Large-cap ETFs focus on stocks of companies with a market capitalization typically exceeding $10 billion. Some of the leading large-cap ETFs in the US are SPDR S&P 500 ETF Trust (SPY) ($564.4 billion AUM), iShares Core S&P 500 ETF (IVV) ($528.4 billion AUM), and Vanguard S&P 500 ETF (VOO) ($517 billion). These are also the top 3 equity ETFs in the US based on AUM.

There are also several other types of equity ETFs based on:

◇ **Investment style - active vs. passive**: For example, Vanguard S&P 500 ETF (VOO) (passive or index ETF) and JPMorgan Equity Premium Income ETF (JEPI) (active ETF)

◇ **Sectoral exposure**: For example, Energy Select Sector SPDR Fund (XLE) and iShares U.S. Home Construction ETF (ITB).

◇ **Investment theme**: For example, ARK Innovation ETF (ARKK) (investing in disruptive and futuristic technology) and Vanguard Dividend Appreciation ETF (VIG).

◇ **Regional exposure**: For example, Vanguard FTSE Emerging Markets ETF (VWO).

2. Bond ETFs

Bond ETFs, also called fixed-income ETFs, invest in a basket of national or international government, corporate and municipal bonds. Similar to equity index ETFs, most bond ETFs also track an index such as the Bloomberg U.S. Aggregate Bond Index.

Bond ETFs are available in various types, based on factors like the issuers (government or corporate bond ETFs), geography (national, international, emerging market bonds), credit ratings (investment grade bonds and junk bonds), duration (short-term vs. long term), and invest style (index ETFs or active bond ETFs).

One advantage of bond ETFs is that many of them pay monthly dividends based on the interest income earned on the bonds held in the fund's portfolio.

This makes Bond ETFs ideal for conservative investors and those looking for regular income from their investments, whereas stock ETFs are better suited for long-term investors aiming for growth over time. Moreover, Bond ETFs are a cost-effective solution to diversify your portfolio.

Here are the 3 largest Bond ETFs in the US:

1. **iShares Core U.S. Aggregate Bond ETF (AGG)**: Total assets - $120.9 billion

2. **Vanguard Total Bond Market ETF (BND)**: Total assets - $118.6 billion

3. **iShares 20+ Year Treasury Bond ETF (TLT)**: Total assets - $62.8

3. Sector and industry ETFs

Sector and industry ETFs allow you to focus on the most promising and high-growth areas of the economy. So if you think the tech sector is outperforming others (which has been the case for the last few years), buying a tech-specific ETF (for example, Vanguard Information Technology ETF (VGT), VanEck Semiconductor ETF (SMH), or iShares U.S. Technology ETF (IYW)) can help you leverage this fast-growing sector.

However, remember that while one sector may look promising today, it can soon go out of fashion while another sector may start performing better, turning the entire endeavor into an endless cat-and-mouse game due to sector rotation. For instance, after a solid bull run between 2017-21, many solar and clean energy ETFs started underperforming in the last 3 years. Therefore, in the long run, broader index ETFs (such as the S&P 500 ETFs) may be more effective for most passive investors.

Here are some of the leading sectoral ETFs in the US:

◇ **Technology**: Vanguard Information Technology ETF (VGT)

◇ **Financials**: Financial Select Sector SPDR Fund (XLF)

◇ **Healthcare**: Health Care Select Sector SPDR Fund (XLV)

4. International ETFs

These ETFs invest in stocks, bonds, real estate, and other assets in foreign markets. Intentional ETFs offer cost-effective ways to diversify one's investments beyond national boundaries and profit from high-growth economies and industries abroad. The focus of international ETFs can be as broad as the entire global market (for example: iShares MSCI World ETF) or the European market (Vanguard FTSE Europe ETF) and as specific as small-cap stocks in Brazil (VanEck Brazil Small-Cap ETF).

Here are some prominent international ETFs:

◇ **Vanguard FTSE Developed Markets ETF (VEA)**: Invests in a diversified group of large, mid, and small-cap companies located in Canada and the major markets of Europe and the Pacific region.

◇ **iShares Core MSCI EAFE ETF (IEFA)**: Focuses on large-, mid-, and small-cap developed market equities, excluding the U.S. and Canada.

◇ **SPDR Portfolio Developed World ex-US ETF (SPDW)**: Offers broad exposure to developed market equities outside the United States.

5. Commodity ETFs

Commodities like gold are traditionally considered effective hedges against stock market downturns. Commodity ETFs invest in a diverse range of assets like gold, silver, oil, other precious metals, and agricultural products. A commodity ETF can invest in a specific commodity (for example, SPDR Gold Shares and iShares Silver Trust) or a basket of commodities (for example, First Trust Global Tactical Commodity Strategy Fund).

These ETFs get exposure to commodities through several means such as investing in physical commodities (for example, iShares Gold Trust) or investing in stocks of companies that produce, transport, and store commodities (for instance, VenEck Gold Miners ETF). Investing in an ETF that contains physical commodities is akin to investing in physical gold or silver but without the pain of purchasing, ensuring quality and securely storing the actual assets.

Some of the leading commodity ETFs in the US are:

◇ SPDR Gold Trust (GLD)

◇ iShares Gold Trust (IAU)

◇ iShares Silver Trust (SLV)

6. Real estate ETFs

Real Estate ETFs invest in the real estate market through various modes. Most commonly, real estate ETFs invest in Real Estate Investment Trusts (REITs), which are legal entities that own, operate, or finance income-producing real estate.

Real estate ETFs offer a simpler and cost-effective way to get exposure to the real estate market without owning physical properties. Here are some of the leading real-estate ETFs in the US:

◇ Vanguard Real Estate ETF (VNQ)

◇ Real Estate Select Sector SPDR Fund (XLRE)

◇ Schwab US REIT ETF (SCHH)

7. Thematic and Specialty ETFs

Consider some of the most exciting investment themes of today. You might be thinking of electric vehicles, semiconductors, artificial intelligence, cryptocurrency, and renewable energy. Now, what if we can invest in a basket of assets related to these themes? This is what thematic and specialty ETFs do.

They invest in emerging and futuristic investment themes, sectors, and trends. For instance, after much deliberation by the Securities and Exchange Commission (SEC), Bitcoin spot ETFs were allowed in January 2024. Diversifying into emerging investing themes like crypto can help investors experiment with high-growth areas with a small percentage of their investible funds.

Here are some examples of thematic ETFs:

◇ iShares Global Clean Energy ETF (ICLN)

◇ iShares Semiconductor ETF (SOXX)

◇ ARK Innovation ETF (ARKK)

◇ Grayscale Bitcoin Trust (GBTC)

Despite the possibilities of asymmetric return, however, remember that thematic ETFs involve a higher degree of risk as these ETFs bet on the expected future potential rather than a proven financial track record of the underlying assets.

Wrapping it up

ETFs, growing from tiny acorns to mighty oaks in just three decades, have democratized investing by empowering retail investors to participate in diversified asset classes around the world. With thousands of ETFs—covering broad global markets at one end and specific sectors at the other— there is now an ETF for every investor or every investing philosophy.

All you need to do is find the ones that you can stick to in the long run.

Chapter 4

NAVIGATING THE ETF SUPERMARKET

*"The ETF industry has become like a supermarket. You can't go in
and not know what you want—you'll end up buying all these things
that you won't ever eat."*
- **Matthew Reiner**, CEO of Wela Strategies.

In the late 18th and early 19th centuries, as the Irish economy
boomed, there was an increasing demand for food. However, with
agricultural land in short supply, the nation's food security became
heavily dependent on a single crop: the humble potato. Its rapid growth
and adaptability to Ireland's damp, temperate climate made it a favored
choice.

By 1800, the potato had become a key food for 1 in 3 Irish people,
especially during the winter months. Over time, it turned into a year-
round staple for farmers and the low-income population. But lurking
beneath the surface was a great danger: the Irish people not only
depended on a single crop, they were also mainly cultivating just one
genetic variety—the Irish Lumper potato. It was monoculture at its
peak!

In the 1840s, Ireland's uniform potato crops fell victim to a devastating
fungus known as potato blight. This blight destroyed the Lumper
variety, leading to a sudden and complete crop failure. Irish farmers
had no backup varieties to deal with the crisis. Between 1845 and 1852,
over a million Irish people perished from starvation, while more than

two million fled the country to escape hunger.

Figure 11: *A destitute family during the Irish famine of the 1840s (Source: The Pictorial Times)*

This prolonged period of starvation and disease, known as the "Irish Potato Famine," highlights the dangers of depending on a single crop variety. Monoculture increases vulnerability to diseases. The Irish Potato Famine, however, offers a crucial lesson about investing—the importance of diversification.

A few words about diversification

Diversification implies that relying entirely on one option (or, putting all your eggs in the same basket) is a bad idea. In investing, you can diversify by spreading your capital across multiple assets. This will help you manage risks (hoping that when one asset class tanks, the others can recoup the losses) and optimize return. For instance, as stocks are riskier than bonds, traditionally investors have included stocks and bonds in their portfolios in certain ratios (60:40 being the classic portfolio distribution) to diversify.

A basic rule of diversification is to invest in assets that are negatively correlated or have little to no correlation with each other. When two assets have a negative correlation, the price of one tends to rise as the other falls. For example, when oil prices increase, airline stocks often decline in value (higher oil prices mean increased operational costs and lower profits for airlines). Similarly, when you invest in unrelated assets, their prices move independently. In both cases, you can derive the benefits of diversification.

However, when different assets have a positive correlation—meaning they move in the same direction—your entire portfolio becomes more vulnerable to risk. For example, if your investments are heavily concentrated in tech stocks, any negative news affecting the sector, such as strict regulations or supply chain disruptions, could significantly impact your entire portfolio. So, while investing in high-growth sectors like tech, you can mitigate risks by diversifying into defensive sectors like utilities or pharmaceuticals.

Does the traditional stock-bond diversification strategy still hold up?

While the underlying concept of diversification is straightforward, it's a little more nuanced in practice. One reason is that the correlation of assets may change over time because of many complex factors. For instance, the correlation between two leading asset classes—stocks and bonds—has widely fluctuated over the last three and half decades.

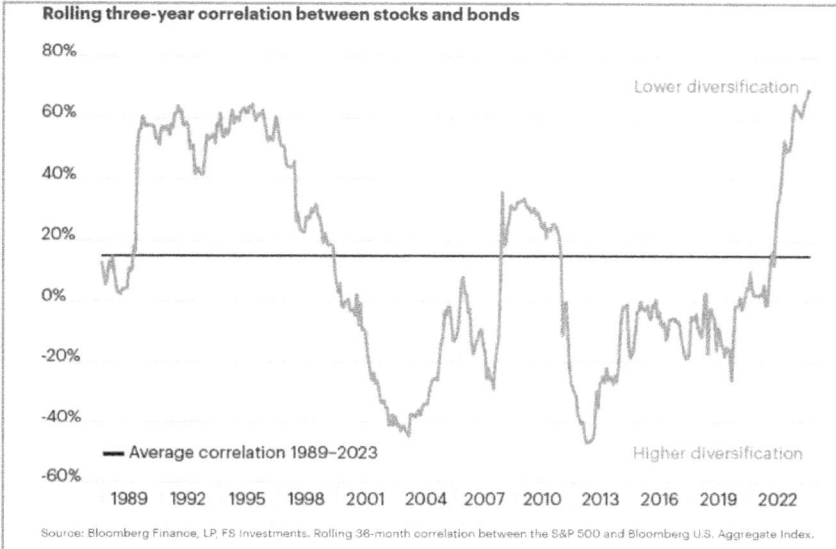

Figure 12: *Fluctuating correlation between stocks and bonds (Source: Bloomberg Finance)*

As of December 31, 2023, the three-year correlation between stocks and bonds spiked to a nearly four-decade high level of 0.68. This means that bonds no longer offer the same diversification benefits as before. When the stock market falls, bonds too are likely to crash due to the strongly positive correlation (we observed the same during the 2022 stock market decline when both stocks and bond prices fell).

However, the good news is that a broad index-based stock portfolio, for instance, the Vanguard Total Stock Market ETF (VTI) beats all other asset mixes over the long run. Here is how, according to Morningstar Direct, different combinations of stocks and bonds performed over the past 30 years (as of July 2023):

Growth of $100 for Various Asset Mixes over the Past 30 Years

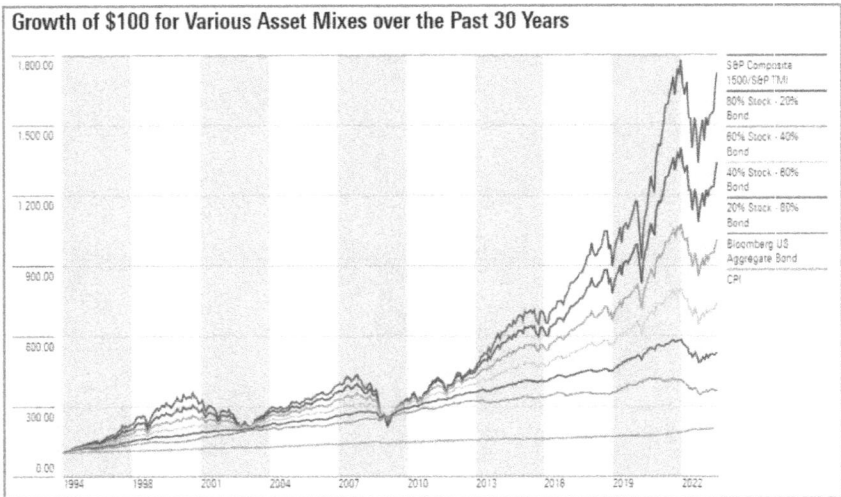

Figure 13: *Growth of $100 for different equity-bond combinations (Source: Morningstar Direct)*

As you can see in the figure above, the S&P Composite 1500 (includes all stocks in the S&P 500, S&P 400, and S&P 600, covering 90% of the entire US stock market valuation), outperformed all other portfolios comprising stocks and bonds in the last 3 decades. The chart also shows two important things:

1. When the investment horizon is sufficiently long, stocks typically recover from big crashes, such as the dot-com bubble, the 2008 global financial crisis, or the shock from the 2020 pandemic.

2. During those market shocks, portfolios containing a higher proportion of bonds experienced less damage than those heavily invested in stocks. However, stocks eventually regained their losses over the following years and significantly outperformed bonds in the long run.

Your diversification strategy largely depends on your investment goals, the duration you plan to invest, and your risk tolerance. However, if you don't need to access a large portion of your funds for some time, ideally a greater percentage of your portfolio should consist of stocks.

ETFs, especially the ones tracking broad indices, offer excellent diversification. An ETF-only portfolio (or even an equity ETF-only portfolio) can serve all your diversification needs as ETFs hold diversified assets. For example, the Vanguard Total World Stock ETF (VT) holds around 9,000 stocks across more than 47 countries, encompassing both developed and emerging markets. It captures over 98% of the global investable market capitalization. As of October 31, 2024, VT has delivered an average annual return of 11.03% over the past 5 years and 9.12% over the last 10 years.

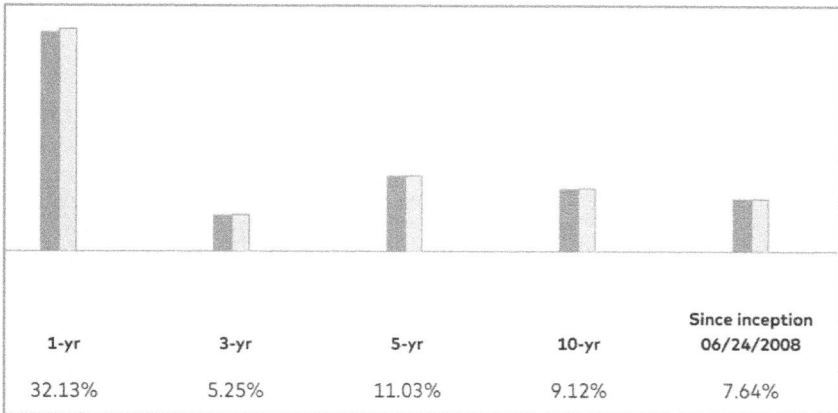

Figure 14: Average annual returns of Vanguard Total World Stock ETF (VT) (Source: investor.vanguard.com)

Now, let's now explore some common strategies for creating an ETF-only portfolio.

Different approaches to building an ETF-only portfolio

The global ETF market offers a buffet from which you can choose what you like based on your investment objectives, risk tolerance level, and investment horizon. Here are standard approaches to choosing ETFs for your long-term portfolio.

The 3-Fund Portfolio for the Bogleheads

"Bogleheads" refers to the investing community who follow the investment philosophy of Jack Bogle, the founder of Vanguard and pioneer of index fund investing. They focus on low-cost investing, broad diversification, and a long-term approach to wealth building.

The 3-fund portfolio popularized by the Bogleheads typically consists of:

1. **U.S. Stock ETF**: Provides exposure to the U.S. equity market. Example: Vanguard S&P 500 ETF (VOO).

2. **International Stock ETF**: Covers developed and emerging markets outside the US. Example: Vanguard Total International Stock ETF (VXUS).

3. **Bond ETF**: Offers fixed-income exposure to balance risk and enhance stability. Example: Vanguard Total Bond Market Index Fund (BND)

The allocation ratio between stocks (including U.S. and international stocks) and bonds depends on your risk profile. A common rule of thumb is that the percentage of stocks in your portfolio should equal 100 minus your age. For instance, if you are 35, this would suggest that 65% of your capital should be invested in equity ETFs.

However, it's important to note that bonds may not provide the same level of diversification they once did. Therefore, it can be a more effective strategy to allocate a much higher percentage towards stocks. Moreover, the global vs. US stock allocation is a much less critical decision as US and international stocks show similar risk profiles and returns over the long term.

Here is a sample 3-fund portfolio with 3 ETFs:

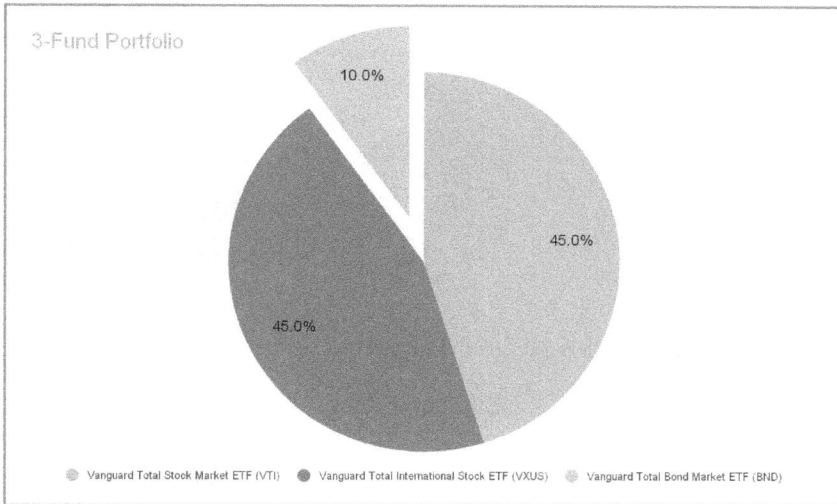

Figure 15: *A sample 3-Fund portfolio*

(Note: These ETFs are only indicative and we don't recommend any specific ETFs).

The core-satellite strategy

In this strategy, a larger portion of capital is invested in a long-term core portfolio whereas a smaller portion is allocated towards trending sectors for the short run. Traditionally, the core-satellite strategy combines the advantages of index funds—such as lower costs, greater diversification, tax efficiency, and reduced volatility—with actively managed funds or other direct investments that have the potential for higher returns.

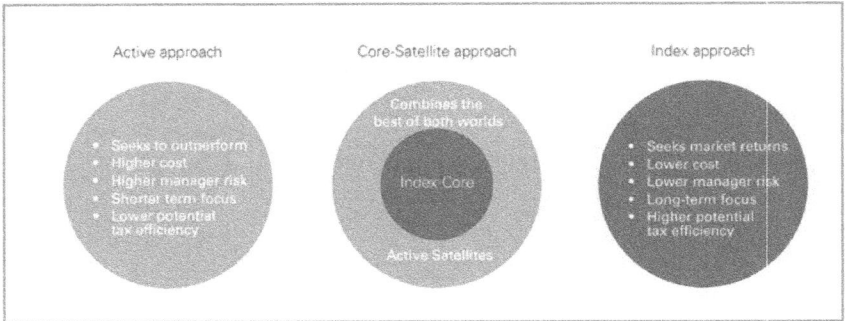

Figure 16: Core-satellite strategy (Source: vanguard.com.au)

To adopt this approach in ETF investing, you can establish a core holding of low-cost, broad-market ETFs (for instance, ETFs targeting the entire US market or the global market) to provide stability and diversification. 80% of your capital goes to the core component. Now complement this core with sector-specific or thematic ETFs (for instance, Financial Select Sector SPDR Fund (XLF) or ARK Innovation ETF (ARKK)) as satellites to pursue higher returns.

Now let's look at a portfolio that can generate relatively stable returns across all economic weathers: recession, economic growth, inflation, or deflation.

Ray Dalio's All-Weather Portfolio

Back in the 1970s, Ray Dalio (a legendary investor, hedge fund manager, and the founder of Bridgewater Associates, the world's largest hedge fund) was exploring a question:

"What kind of investment portfolio would you hold that would perform well across all environments, be it a devaluation or something completely different?"

After decades of research, Dalio found his answer and the result was his all-weather investment strategy. The concept behind this strategy was that different asset classes have different correlations with each other. Therefore, they respond in unique ways to different economic conditions, such as inflation or recession.

The typical allocation in this strategy involves 5 asset classes:

◇ 30% US stocks

◇ 40% Long-Term bonds

◇ 15% Intermediate-term bonds

◇ 7.5% Gold

◇ 7.5% Commodities

Between March 2005 and July 2024, the Ray Dalio All Weather Portfolio delivered a compound annual growth rate (CAGR) of 6.62% compared to 10.38% by the S&P 500. However, its maximum drawdown in this period was 21.4% compared to 51% for the S&P 500.

We can replicate this strategy using ETFs in the following manner:

◇ **30% in a total equity market** - Example: Vanguard Total World Stock ETF (VT))

◇ **40% in a long-term bond ETF** - Example: iShares 20+ Year Treasury Bond ETF (TLT)

◇ **15% in an intermediate-term bond ETF** - Example: Vanguard Intermediate-Term Bond ETF (BIV)

◇ **7.5% in a gold ETF** - Example: SPDR Gold Trust (GLD)

◇ **7.5% in a commodity ETF** - (Example: Invesco DB Commodity Index Tracking Fund)

In addition to the portfolio approaches discussed above, here are some other strategies to experiment with:

1. **The Coffeehouse Portfolio**: Given by Wall Street veteran Bill Schultheis, this passive investing strategy allocates:

   i. 50% in equities

      a. 10% large-cap blend ((Invesco S&P 500® Equal Weight ETF (RSP))

      b. 10% large-cap value ((Vanguard Value ETF (VTV))

    c.   10% small-cap blend ((iShares Core S&P Small-Cap ETF (IJR))

    d.   10% small-cap value ((Vanguard Small Cap Value ETF (VBR))

   ii. 40% in intermediate bonds ((Vanguard Intermediate-Term Bond ETF (BIV))

   iii. 10% in Real estate investment trusts (REITs) ((Vanguard Real Estate ETF (VNQ))

2. **Pure passive income**: If generating steady passive income is your goal, you can consider investing in dividend-focused ETFs like iShares Core High Dividend ETF (HDV) and option strategy ETFs like Global X NASDAQ 100 Covered Call ETF (QYLD) or JPMorgan Equity Premium Income ETF (JEPI). Dividend ETFs make periodic dividend payments earned by the fund from the underlying stocks. Option strategy ETFs generate a steady income through a variety of strategies such as covered call (holding a long position in a stock and then selling call options on the same stock).

3. **Keep it simple**: If you want to keep things really simple, you can create a balanced, diversified portfolio of stocks and bonds using just 2 ETFs: a total world stock market ETF and a total bond market ETF.

Wrapping it up

One of the key principles of risk management, both in life and investing, is the importance of diversification. ETFs follow this idea by empowering investors to buy the entire haystack instead of hunting for a single needle within it. No longer do you need to depend on just one variety of potatoes; ETFs provide a buffet of options. You can take the diversification game to the next level by choosing ETFs from different asset classes, sectors, or geographies.

Diversification doesn't get any better than this.

Chapter 5

GETTING STARTED WITH ETF INVESTING

"The best time to plant a tree was 20 years ago.
The next best time is today."
*- **Chinese Proverb.***

As of October 2024, Warren Buffett, 94, is the 9th richest individual on Earth, with a net worth of approximately $144 billion. However, the Oracle of Omaha was not even a billionaire until he turned 56. 99% of his entire wealth came after crossing 50 years of age (even though Buffett bought his first stock at the age of 11). Based on 2022 data, the average age of billionaires worldwide is between 50 and 70. Over 40% of these mega-rich people were older than 70.

These data show that building a significant amount of wealth is often a result of years, or even decades, of disciplined investing. There is another key lesson that you must not miss: the importance of starting now.

However, the most tricky thing about getting started is taking the very first step. It's rather easier to procrastinate when faced with a big goal. But as Mark Twain said:

"The secret of getting started is breaking your complex
overwhelming tasks into small manageable tasks, and starting on
the first one."

Let's just do that to kick off your first ETF investment.

If you've made it this far in the book, you've probably made up your mind to invest in ETFs. The first 4 chapters of this book set the stage and give an overview of how ETFs can help common investors build slow wealth (with faster routes often leading to disasters) over the long run. Let's now get down to the specifics of how to start investing in ETFs.

Setting up your investment account

To begin with, you need a brokerage account to buy ETFs. It's great if you already have one for trading stocks. Most stock brokers (for example, Charles Schwab, Fidelity, and Interactive Brokers) offer an array of ETFs. It may be more convenient for beginners with small investment sizes to stick to a single broker for trading different asset classes like stocks, bonds, commodities, and of course, ETFs.

If you don't have a brokerage account, no worries - it's super convenient to open a brokerage account online with any of the leading brokerage firms in about 15 minutes. Some of the leading ETF brokers include:

◇ Fidelity

◇ Interactive Brokers

◇ Charles Schwab

◇ Vanguard

◇ Freetrade (UK)

◇ Wealthsimple (Canada)

◇ Zerodha (India)

Typically, you will be asked to provide your government-issued ID, tax identity number, and proof of identity when opening a brokerage account. Once your account is approved, you can fund it and start buying your first ETF. Many brokers allow you to invest with as little as $1.

Note that in addition to the above-mentioned traditional brokers, there is a new class of online platforms called "robo advisors" (examples: Wealthfront and Betterment Digital) which automates investing for you. If you want a hands-off approach to investing, robo-advisors can replicate your investment style based on your preferences. It builds, monitors, and automatically rebalances your portfolio based on market conditions. Moreover, many traditional brokers such as Charles Schwab offer robo-advisor services (these come with additional costs) for their clients to automate fund selection and portfolio rebalancing.

While opening a brokerage account, compare different brokers based on factors like <u>fees, minimum deposits, types of securities traded</u> (stocks, bonds, ETFs, and crypto), <u>customer service</u>, and <u>whether or not they allow fractional investing </u>(this means you can buy a fraction of an ETF's share) and <u>regulatory status</u> (don't fall for illegitimate, fly-by-night brokers<u>)</u>. Among these factors, fees and charges (which may include account opening, maintenance, and trading fees) are probably the most important factors affecting your net investment returns.

While ETFs have a low expense ratio, there may be other associated costs of trading frequently. Many online brokers don't charge any account maintenance fees or ETF trading commissions. However, there can be other charges such as service fees. To sum it all up: look for reputed brokers with low or no costs for maintaining your account or trading ETFs.

Buying your first ETF

Once your brokerage account is activated (which may take a couple of hours to a couple of days post-application), you are all set to buy your first ETF. Most ETF brokers provide an ETF research tool, like a database to search ETFs of your choice. Using this database, you can check several important details such as expense ratio, the assets under an ETF, and its historical performance.

Alternatively, you can check out online ETF screeners like etfdb.com or stockanalysis.com to screen ETFs using different criteria (asset types, region, market cap, and AUM). Lastly, you can check all relevant information about an ETF (constituents, performance, expense ratio, volatility, and dividend-related information) on the official websites of respective ETF issuers.

For beginners, our advice is to buy broad market ETFs like the following:

◇ **Vanguard S&P 500 ETF (VOO)** - Expense ratio: 0.03%, 10-year average annual return: 13.33% (as of 30 Sept, 2024)

◇ **Vanguard Total Stock Market ETF (VTI):** Expense ratio 0.03%, 10-year average annual return 12.78% (as of 30 Sept 2024)

◇ **Vanguard Total World Stock ETF (VT):** Expense ratio: 0.07%, 10-year average annual return: 9.49% (as of 30 Sept 2024)

Their broad market exposure, low cost, and strong track record make them great candidates for your first ETF. Let's now look at a comprehensive checklist for buying ETFs.

> **Note**: This is only an indicative list and we don't make any recommendations to invest in a particular ETF.

Checklist for buying your first ETF

Look at these factors while deciding on which ETFs to buy:

◇ **Expense ratio**: Look for ETFs with low expense ratios. Even a slightly higher expense ratio can significantly erode returns over time. Note that different ETFs tracking the same index may have different expense ratios. For instance, the Vanguard S&P 500 ETF (VOO) has an expense ratio of 0.03%, whereas the SPDR S&P 500 ETF Trust has an expense ratio of 0.09%. The differences may seem minimal, but there's no reason to leave money on the table. With everything else being equal, the fund with the lower fee is clearly more aligned with investors' best interests.

◇ **Liquidity**: Look for highly liquid ETFs (check for average trading volume, asset under management (AUM), and the liquidity of the underlying assets) to ensure you can buy/sell ETFs easily.

◇ **Tracking errors**: It reflect how close the return of an ETF follows the return of the index tracks. For instance, an ETF tracking the S&P 500 should match the return of the S&P by an exact percentage. However, tracking errors (which can happen due to several reasons such as portfolio rebalancing by the ETF sponsor, management expenses, and sampling - some ETFs may choose to invest in a representative sample of an index rather than holding all the index components) can be a deviation between their returns. Look for funds with lower tracking errors.

◇ **Fund size**: Larger funds generally have more liquidity and may be less likely to close (an ETF sponsor may choose to close an ETF because of a lack of investor interest or poor returns. In case that happens, shareholders receive a distribution proportional to their investment in the ETF).

◇ **Provider reputation**: Choose ETFs from reputable providers with a history of good management. Some of the most reputed ETF sponsors include Vanguard, State Street Global Advisors (SPDR ETFs), BlackRock (iShares), Invesco, Van Eck, and Fidelity.

◇ **Diversification and exposure**: Assess the ETF's exposure to different sectors or regions to ensure diversification.

ETF redundancy: avoiding overlap in your portfolio

Different ETFs may be tracking the same index. For instance, the Vanguard S&P 500 ETF (VOO) and SPDR S&P 500 ETF Trust (SPY) have the exact same components: all the S&P 500 stocks. Therefore, buying both these ETFs is like buying the same bucket of assets from different sellers.

Moreover, even though two ETFs may not have the same components, significant overlapping can exist. For instance, if we compare Vanguard Total Stock Market ETF (VTI) and SPDR S&P 500 ETF Trust (SPY), both include major US large-cap stocks. Investing in ETFs with the same or similar components exposes you to the same risk-return profile. Therefore, while buying an ETF look for their components to ensure that you don't invest in overlapping ETFs. In this regard, one key advantage of ETFs is that, unlike mutual funds, most ETFs disclose their holdings daily.

How many ETFs to buy?

First of all, there's no one-size-fits-all rule for the ideal number of ETFs in your portfolio. The right amount depends on your investment style, overall portfolio diversification strategy (discussed in Chapter 04), risk tolerance, and how actively you want to manage your investments (Remember, having more ETFs requires more time for research and monitoring). A common rule of thumb is that fewer ETFs can be better. If you want to invest only in equities, 2 ETFs (one each for US and global equities) or even 1 (tracking the S&P 500) can be enough. However, if you want exposure to other assets like bonds, commodities, and thematic ETFs, you may need to buy 3-8 ETFs.

One of the main advantages of purchasing ETFs over individual stocks is that they allow you to simplify tracking your portfolio. Instead of managing 20 or 50 different stocks, you only need to monitor a single ETF. This makes it much easier to stay on top of your investments. Buying too many ETFs not only makes it difficult to track them all (with their hundreds and even thousands of components), but it also increases the risks of overlapping.

Wrapping it up

One common investing mistake is putting your money in the wrong assets. However, an even bigger mistake is not investing at all. Investing lets your money work for you, even when you're not. Remember, any amount is a good amount to start investing.

And, the best time to invest is now!

Chapter 6

NOT TOO OFTEN, NOT TOO RARELY -
THE ART OF REBALANCING YOUR ETF
PORTFOLIO

"Value stocks are about as exciting as watching grass grow, but have you ever noticed just how much your grass grows in a week?"
- Christopher Browne.

Picture this: one day, you log into your brokerage account—most likely through an investing app—and check the market's performance for the day. What is the likelihood that you'll observe a market decline rather than a positive performance on an average day? (According to a study by CNBC Select and Dynata, 49% of investors track their portfolio daily!).

Studies indicate that there is approximately a 46% chance of the market declining, meaning it falls almost every other day!

Now what if you look at the market monthly, quarterly, semi-annually, or annually? The probability that the market declined in the previous period now falls to 38%, 32%, 26%, and 21% respectively. And what if you check the market just once in 20 years? What could be the likelihood that the market will generate negative returns in 20 years?

Market data between 1926 and 2015 shows that the number of times the S&P 500 declined in any rolling 20-year period is precisely equal to zero!

Well, we are in no way suggesting that you should invest and then live under a rock for the next two decades without checking your portfolio. What past market data suggests is that the more frequently we look at our portfolios, the higher the chance of experiencing a market decline, which leads to bad investment decisions driven by hasty emotional reactions. It means when we are strongly focused on the short-term, we tend to react too negatively to recent losses, at the cost of long-term benefits.

Academicians call this tendency *myopic loss aversion*. In their paper, ***Myopic Loss Aversion and the Equity Premium Puzzle***, researchers Shlomo Benartzi and Richard Thaler introduced this concept. They concluded, "The longer the investor intends to hold the asset, the more attractive the risky asset will appear, as long as the investment is not evaluated frequently."

This means the more we tune out the daily ups and downs of the market, the easier it is to stick to our long-term investment goals. According to Dan Egan:

> *"Looking at your portfolio frequently can make you feel like it's performing worse than it actually is, and the less likely you'll invest correctly for long-term success."*

So, how often should we check out portfolios or make periodic adjustments? Let's look for an answer. But before that, here are a few words about why you may need to rebalance at all.

Rebalancing vs. timing the market

When you start out to invest, you build a portfolio based on several factors like your financial goals, age, income, investment horizon, and risk tolerance. However, since life is not static, your investment philosophy may change with changing circumstances, new life events (for instance, getting married, having children, or approaching retirement), changes in income, or a renewed take on risk tolerance.

Additionally, your investment horizon is always shrinking. If you started five years ago with an investment horizon of a decade, now you are left with only 5 years to achieve your goals. While approaching retirement, people may value stability over mixing return. Moreover, there can be structural changes in the business environment, economy, or even a major shift in geopolitics (changing the payoffs of different asset classes in different regions). Long-term policy shifts (for instance, major policy changes favoring an economic sector like renewable energy) may make one sector more investment-worthy than others.

Plus, changes in asset prices can drift your asset accumulation too far from your target. For example, imagine you began investing ten years ago with a 70:30 stock-to-bond portfolio. Now since stocks tend to perform better than bonds in the long run, because of price appreciation, your 70% stock, and 30% bond portfolio may have drifted to 90% stocks and 10% bonds. It's time to make some adjustments to align your asset allocations with your original 70:30 stock-to-bond portfolio.

Research by Vanguard shows that a portfolio consisting of 60% equities and 40% fixed income at the end of 1989 if left unbalanced, would have shifted to 80% equities by the end of 2021.

Figure 17: *Asset allocation - never rebalanced vs. annually rebalanced (Source: Vanguard)*

In short, when there is a change in your overall investment goals or life circumstances, it's probably a good time to have a look at your asset mix and evaluate whether it still works for you. Portfolio rebalancing is the process of buying and selling portions of your investments to restore the weight of each asset class to its pre-determined allocation or make adjustments to your portfolio based on changing circumstances.

However, remember that rebalancing is not the same as timing the market. When investors try to time the market (which is a bad long-term strategy), they try to predict market tops and bottoms. In rebalancing, however, our goal is to make adjustments to our portfolios to align them with our investment goals. Portfolio rebalancing is not a short-term strategy to maximize return but a systemic procedure to manage risks and achieve long-term (five years or more) investment goals.

How often do you rebalance your portfolio?

As we just discussed, constantly monitoring short-term returns can lead to impulsive reactions and hasty decision-making, which will not allow your money to grow over time.

61

Research by Vanguard shows that the optimal rebalancing methods are neither too frequent (for example, weekly, monthly, or even quarterly) nor too infrequent (for example once every 2-3 years). Although not a rule of thumb, for most investors the optimal rebalancing frequency is once a year.

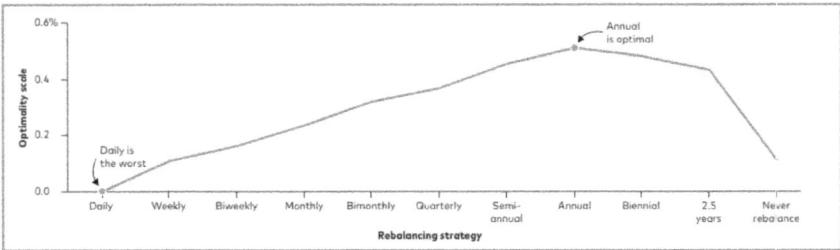

Figure 18: *Optimal portfolio rebalancing frequency (Source: https://corporate.vanguard.com/)*

Remember that there should be a strong trigger (for example, your risk profile changed) or a system (you rebalance when a particular asset class achieves a certain investment goal like appreciating 25%) behind portfolio rebalancing. It can neither be random nor an activity to kill boredom! Charlie Munger said, "The first rule of compounding: Never interrupt it unnecessarily,"

Key Metrics

While tracking your ETF portfolio, keep an eye on various indicators like performance, expense ratio, and turnover rates (how frequently assets an ETF are bought and sold by the ETF sponsor). Here are some target expense ratios to look for in different types of ETFs:

◇ **Broad market index** - <0.1% (Example: Vanguard S&P 500 ETF (VOO), Expense ratio: 0.03%)

◇ **Sector ETF** - <0.25% (Example: Technology Select Sector SPDR Fund (XLK), Expense ratio: 0.09%)

◇ **Geographic ETF** - <0.3% (Example: iShares Core MSCI Emerging Markets ETF (IEMG), Expense ratio: 0.09%)

◇ **Thematic ETF** - <0.5% (Example: iShares Electric Vehicles and Driving Technology UCITS ETF (ECAR), Expense ratio: 0.40%)

When the expense ratio of an ETF goes up, it may be a good reason to switch to similar ETFs offering similar returns at lower expenses.

Note that rebalancing your ETFs may attract capital gain taxes when you book profits. Therefore, taxation is an important consideration while rebalancing your portfolio (discussed in more detail in Chapter 08).

2 Rebalancing methods

2 of the most common methods to rebalance your ETF portfolio are **1. Calendar-based rebalancing** and, **2. Threshold-based rebalancing**. Following the first method, you can rebalance your ETF portfolio on fixed periodic intervals (for instance, quarterly or annually).

In the second method, rebalancing is done when your portfolio experiences a change in its asset allocation exceeding a certain threshold. For instance, if you don't want more than 70% of your portfolio to be invested in equity ETFs (and your threshold is 5%), you can consider rebalancing whenever the equity component goes over 75%.

Handling market volatility

Prolific American investor Howard Marks said, "Emotion is one of the investor's greatest enemies." Nothing disrupts long-term investment results more than emotional reactions by investors triggered by market volatility. In a Morningstar article, columnist Ben Johnson says:

> *"When markets are tough, don't look. When market volatility ticks up, investors may be best served by tuning out".*

According to studies on myopic loss aversion, an investor who reviews their portfolio quarterly rather than daily can decrease the likelihood of experiencing a moderate loss (defined as -2% or more) from 25% to 12%. <u>The key to dealing with market volatility is not checking your portfolio daily</u>. If your investment horizon spans 10 to 20 years, short-term market fluctuations are merely noise and should not influence your decisions.

Volatility is the inherent nature of the market. Every couple of years, the market may go down 10-30% or even more. In the 20 years between 2002 and 2021, a market drawdown of 10% or more occurred in 10 out of 20 years, or 50% of the time. However, panic selling at the bottom would have driven you out of the market and you would have missed the subsequent recoveries (imagine selling at the bottom during the pandemic-induced market crash and staying out of the market for the next 2-3 years - you would have missed one of the steepest bull-runs in recent history!)

Wrapping it up

ETFs are long-term investment tools. Periodic rebalancing may be required to adjust your portfolio with a set of dynamic factors. However, rebalancing should not be an excuse to time the market. Over the long term, the market will handle much of the heavy lifting for us, as long as we stay invested and ride the waves. Some tweaks along the way can help as long as we have a strong reason or system to do so.

Rebalancing, therefore, should neither be too often nor too rarely!

Chapter 7

ALL THAT GLITTERS IS NOT GOLD

"All that glisters is not gold;
Often have you heard that told:
Many a man his life hath sold
But my outside to behold:
Gilded tombs do worms enfold."
*- **William Shakespeare**, The Merchant of Venice*

Investors trying to beat the market often flock to the small-cap space, believing that's where the next big 10x opportunities can be discovered. The Russell 2000 Index, the small-cap index of choice in the US (tracking the smallest 2,000 securities in the Russell 3000 index), generated a decent 9.4% annualized return in the last 5 years ending Sept 2024. So, an ETF tracking the Russell 2000 Index will likely achieve a similar return. For instance, the iShares Russell 2000 ETF generated an annualized 9.3% return in the same period.

Now, what if an ETF claims to deliver three times the index's return? This is exactly what the Direxion Daily Small Cap Bull 3X ETF (TNA) aims at. Technically, it offers 3X daily leveraged exposure to the Russell 2000 Index. For the average Joe, this means that TNA aims to achieve 300% of the daily performance of this small-cap index.

Considering the Russell 2000's annualized return of 9.4% over the past five years, you might expect the Direxion Daily Small Cap Bull 3X ETF to have delivered an annualized return of around 28%. In reality, it posted an annualized return of -3.9%—that's right, a negative return!

How is that even possible?

We are coming to that point shortly. But before that, let's note a key point: <u>Not all ETFs, not even some shiny ones, are worth it.</u>

In the last one or two decades, the conveyor belt of ETF production has produced a large number of ETFs in all shapes and sizes. Some of which are too complex for the common investors. Or, they simply don't uphold the 'true spirits' of ETFs: cost-effective, hands-off, passive investing tools! In the words of Bloomberg Intelligence's Athanasios Psarofagis:

> *"Kudos for the ETF industry for always pushing the envelope, but some of the new launches seem to go against the value proposition of ETFs being diversified, inexpensive investments, to catering more towards the traders and speculators."*

This chapter talks about the types of ETFs that are no-go zones for long-term investors. Let's dive in.

What's in a name?

Many investors believe that the name of an ETF reflects what it does or what its components are. This may be true for some ETFs—however, for a large number of others, the name may not reflect their components or their true nature. For instance, the SPDR S&P Emerging Middle East & Africa ETF (GAF), which was eventually closed in 2017, allocated 90% of holdings to a single country: South Africa. The remaining 10% was split between Egypt and Morocco. This means the fund pretty much lacked the Middle Eastern exposure its name suggested!

Let's look at another example. When you are buying the VanEck Junior Gold Miners ETF (GDXJ), you are not essentially getting exposure to gold mining companies alone. The fine print says the fund intends to track "...the overall performance of small-capitalization companies that are involved primarily in the mining for gold and/or silver." It's not surprising that Pan American Silver Corp. (which derives one-third of its revenue from silver) is one of its top-10 holdings.

Similarly, there can be "Space ETFs" having a majority of defense companies in their portfolio or "renewable energy ETFs" invested heavily in technology or utility companies marginally attached to the clean-energy space.

Then there are similar-sounding ETF names having significantly different holdings. For instance, look at these 2 similar sounding ETFS: iShares Core MSCI Emerging Markets ETF (IEMG) and iShares MSCI Emerging Markets ETF (EEM). The first one tracks large, mid, and small-cap emerging market equities whereas the second one tracks only large- and mid-cap emerging market equities.

Lastly, there are ETFs like the UBS ETF (LU) Bloomberg US Liquid Corporates UCITS ETF (hedged to EUR) A-acc, a name long enough to confuse the average investor rather than inform them.

In short, the names of many funds don't tell you the whole story. While misleading names may not always lead to significant issues—such as in the case of the VanEck Junior Gold Miners ETF, where there is a strong correlation between the prices of gold and silver—they can create confusion. This confusion may result in an ETF portfolio quite misaligned with your investment goals or risk tolerance So, look for the ETF description, the index it tracks, holdings, and strategies before investing in one.

The problem with leveraged and inverse ETFs

While most ETFs don't invest in derivatives, there is a new breed of ETFs that use derivative instruments to target higher returns. These funds called leveraged ETFs, deploy financial derivatives and debt to amplify the returns of their underlying index and offer 2X or even 3X returns. Similarly, inverse ETFs, which are also leveraged products, amplify the inverse returns of an index (this is akin to taking a leveraged short position on the index - so when the index falls, these ETFs generate 2x or 3x returns).

Just as you guessed it, the Direxion Daily Small Cap Bull 3X ETF (TNA) is a leveraged ETF that promises 300% of the daily returns of the Russell 2000 Index. So, where exactly is the problem?

Well, as they say, the devil lies in the details. Look at the name: Direxion Daily Small Cap Bull 3X ETF (TNA). Here, the keyword is 'Daily'. Most leveraged/inverse ETFs reset their leverage every day. So, when they amplify the ups, even a slight dip in the market can eat out the gains in the long run. Let's look at this example to understand it better:

Let's assume an index and an ETF start at a value of $1,000 and the ETF promises 3X daily returns on the index.

Day 1: The index increases by 5% by the end of the day. So, it closes at $1,050. However, the ETF gains 15% and closes the day at $1,150.

Day 2: The index falls by 5%. So, its value at the day's closure is $997.5. However, the ETF incurs a 15% loss, falling from $1,150 to $977.5.

So, in 2 days, while the index loses only 0.25% (from $1,000 to $997.5), the 3X leveraged ETF ends up losing 2.25% - underperforming the index by a whopping 9x!

This explains how the Direxion Daily Small Cap Bull 3X ETF posted a loss in the last 5 years and not a 28% annualized return (as unsuspecting investors would be tempted to believe looking at the 3X leverage).

However, any investor reading the fine print on the ETF description on its official website could easily avoid all the trouble:

"Investing in a Direxion Shares ETF may be more volatile than investing in broadly diversified funds. The use of leverage by the Fund increases the risk to the Fund. The Direxion Shares ETFs are not suitable for all investors and should be utilized only by sophisticated investors who understand leverage risk and the consequences of seeking daily leveraged investment results and intend to actively monitor and manage their investments."

> **The bottom line**: leveraged and inverse ETFs invest in complex derivate products to achieve the returns they aim for. However, these products may not be suitable for investors looking for stable long-term growth as historically delivered by broader market ETFs like the SPDR S&P 500 ETF Trust (SPY). Moreover, complex ETFs like leveraged or inverse ETFs tend to have high expense ratios, along with high volatility and chances of huge losses. For instance, the Direxion Daily Small Cap Bull 3X Shares (TNA) have an expense ratio of 1.08%! (It wouldn't make the expense ratio cut-off we discussed in Chapter 6.)

When it comes to long-term wealth building through ETFs, what is simple is often better (unless, of course, you are not a short-term trader who thrives on volatility)!

Weight matters

More than 35% of the total market cap of the S&P index (as of July 2024) consists of the "Magnificent Seven": Microsoft, Apple, Nvidia, Alphabet, Amazon, Meta Platforms, and Tesla. These leading technology companies fueled the remarkable market rally following the pandemic.

The S&P 500 index is a market-capitalization-weighted index of the 500 leading publicly traded companies in the U.S. This means the higher the market cap of a firm, the greater the weightage of the firm in the index. This also means the movement of heavyweights like the "Magnificent Seven", has an outsized influence on its performance. For instance, according to Blackrock, the top 20 companies in the S&P 500, contributed more than two-thirds of the index's returns over the past three years.

Market-cap-weighted ETFs have concentration risks as the performance of these ETFs depends on a few big stocks. So, tomorrow if technology stocks go out of favor, the few biggies may pull down the index more than the other 490+ stocks can compensate for. This means if diversification is your top priority, equal-weight ETFs (in which each component stock or asset has an equal representation) can take out some of the concentration risks. In ETFs, concentration risk can emerge whenever it's too tilted towards a few sectors, countries, asset classes, currencies, or investment style

Equal-weighted ETFs, for instance, Invesco S&P 500 Equal Weight ETF (RSP), ensure that each constituent stock has an equal impact on the portfolio's performance, irrespective of its market capitalization.

RSP tracks the S&P 500 Equal Weight Index (EWI), which includes the same constituents of the weighted S&P 500 Index. Each company in the S&P 500 EWI is allocated a fixed weight - or 0.2% of the index. In the last 10 years (Jan 2015 - Sep 2024) RSP clocked an annualized return of 10.5% with a maximum drawdown of 26.7% compared to SPY's annualized return and maximum drawdown of 13.1% and 23.9% respectively. However, since its inception in 2003, RSP has managed to keep pace with SPY with a 9.59% CAGR (compared to 9.65%) by SPY.

Figure 19: *RSP Vs. SPY (Source: https://www.etfcentral.com/)*

Transparency matters

In a recent Financial Times article, ETF correspondent Steve Johnson writes:

> *US regulators approved semi- and non-transparent ETFs in 2019,*
> *paving the way for the structure to depart from the*
> *tried-and-trusted model where ETFs reveal their*
> *full portfolio publicly every day.*

Unlike fully transparent ETFs, semi-transparent ones don't reveal their holdings every day. It's not rocket science to see why these types of ETFs might cut corners and take on higher risks—often beyond what investors are comfortable with—in pursuit of greater returns.

In short, semi-transparent or non-transparent ETFs defy the very purpose of ETFs as a transparent passive investing tool. According to Michael O'Riordan, founding partner of consultancy Blackwater Search and Advisory:

> *"Conceptually, ETFs are meant to be very transparent by their*
> *nature, and now we have introduced something that says it is only*
> *semi-transparent. That's something that goes against the grain."*

It's not uncommon for ETF sponsors to change their strategies overnight, exposing investors to entirely different asset classes and risks. For instance, in 2017, the Tierra XP Latin America Real Estate ETF (LARE), which initially targeted the Latin American real estate market, abruptly shifted its holdings to focus on cannabis companies— an asset class with no conceivable connection to real estate! To ensure transparency and reliability, it's advisable to stick with reputable ETF sponsors such as BlackRock's iShares, Vanguard, State Street, Invesco, VanEck, Global X and Charles Schwab.

Along with avoiding non-transparent ETFs, it's wise to steer clear of ETFs that fail to live up to their hype. For instance, ARK Innovation ETF (ARKK) (Expense ratio: 0.75), was one of the most hyped ETFs following the pandemic. Its holdings include Tesla, Roku, Inc., and Coinbase Global Inc. — companies known for disruptive innovations. However, post-pandemic its performance has been dismal, generating a -25.97% return in the last 3 years.

Similarly, many clean-energy and early-stage tech ETFs experienced a surge during the late 2020 and early 2021 bubble. However, most of them have performed abysmally since then, with many of these ETFs losing half or more of their value as prices corrected. An over-hyped ETF or ETFs targeting a very specific niche (for instance, ETFs geared around Californian carbon permits or Chinese cloud computing) may not be the most suited one for long-term investors looking to survive wild market swings and sectoral shifts. Lastly, avoid unpopular ETFs having very little liquidity.

Wrapping it up

While there is an ETF for almost everything (there is even an ETF named "Inspire 100 ETF (BIBL)", which tracks companies aligned with Biblical values), however not everything with the ETF suffix is worth your money. Broad-based ETFs with a low expense ratio are more likely to align with the needs of long-term investors seeking stable returns and low volatility.

Investing in ETFs that are difficult to understand, lack transparency, are leveraged, or are overhyped can expose you to greater risks than you might want to take on. Some ETFs may appear attractive on the surface but can carry significant risks or fail to align with your investment objectives. The simple rule of thumb is: not everything that glitters is gold and not everything that is gold glitters.

Chapter 8

WHY THE "SMALL" THINGS MATTER

"By the time it came to the edge of the Forest, the stream had grown up, so that it was almost a river, and, being grown-up, it did not run and jump and sparkle along as it used to do when it was younger, but moved more slowly. For it knew now where it was going, and it said to itself, "There is no hurry. We shall get there someday"
*- **A.A. Milne,** The House at Pooh Corner.*

Investing in broad index ETFs is a smart investing strategy, but it comes with a caveat: what if some of the most popular indexes don't translate into the best-performing ETFs? The Dow Jones Industrial Average (DJIA, or simply, "The Dow"), the grandfather of all US indexes, intends to represent the entire US economy but only with 30 stocks (it debuted with just 12 stocks in 1896).

Plus, the Dow is price-weighted. This means that the companies included are chosen based on their stock prices rather than their market capitalizations or overall economic impact. So, UnitedHealth Group Inc. with a stock price of 565.24 (October 29, 2024), commands more than 8.75% weightage in the index, while Apple, with about 7 times the market cap, constitutes only around 3.61%. The top 10 stocks in the Dow represent over 58% of the index's value, highlighting its high concentration risk.

Additionally, while the Dow includes companies like Travelers Cos. Inc. (market cap: $57.29 billion) and 3M (market cap: $70.95 billion), mega-cap giants such as Nvidia (market cap: $3.46 trillion), Alphabet (market cap: $2.10 trillion), and Meta (market cap: $1.50 trillion) are notably absent. Despite its blue-chip ethos and prominence, the Dow is more of a representative of the old economy. This is because the index was created in the 19th century to reflect economic activities in the US and not serve as a benchmark for ETFs, a financial product that would come a century later!

So, Dow-based ETFs (for instance, SPDR Dow Jones Industrial Average ETF (DIA)) fail to offer a worthwhile investment option today in comparison to many broader market ETFs. The latter efficiently channel the market's collective wisdom.

Let's look at this comparison below:

ETF	Benchmark	No. of Holdings	5-Year Avg. Annual Return	10-Year Avg. Annual Return
SPDR Dow Jones Industrial Average ETF Trust (DIA)	Dow Jones	30	11.60%	11.85%
SPDR S&P 500 ETF Trust (SPY)	S&P 500	503	15.82%	13.23%
Vanguard Total Stock Market ETF (VTI)	CRSP US Total Market Index	3654	15.18%	12.78%

Table 2: Comparing DIA, SPY and VTI

Looking closely, 3 of the 4 leading US indexes: the Nasdaq-100, Russell 2000, and the Dow (the exception is the S&P 500) have some inherent issues that make them less effective for ETF investors looking for diversification.

The Nasdaq-100 includes only non-financial stocks and has high concentration risks: as of May 2024, 82% of the index consists of technology (51%), communications (17%), and consumer discretionary stocks (14%). And when it comes to Russell 2000, according to FactSet data, more than 42% of its constituent small-cap companies are loss-makers.

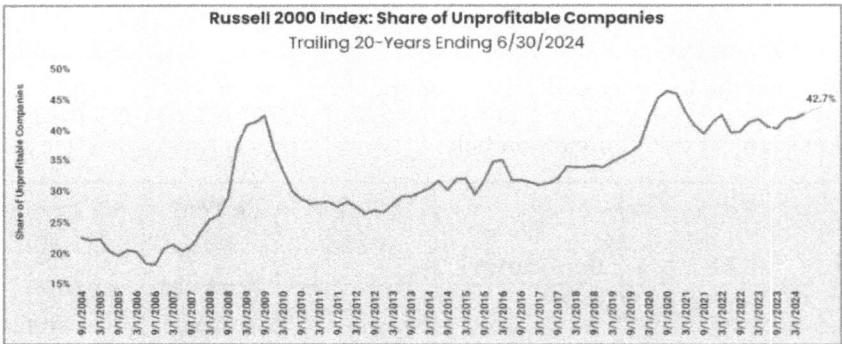

Figure 20: Russell 2000 index: share of loss-making companies (**Source**: Harbor Capital Advisors using data provided by FactSet)

The point we are trying to make is that the popularity of an index alone doesn't make it well-diversified or capable of fulfilling your long-term investment objectives. Also, past performance itself is not a reliable indicator of an index's performance in the future.

For instance, the Invesco QQQ Trust (QQQ), an ETF that tracks the Nasdaq-100 index, has delivered an impressive annualized return of 20.97% over the past five years—an achievement few can match. However, much of this growth has been driven by a rapid surge in tech stocks. It would be unrealistic to expect this exceptional performance to continue in the future.

Therefore, it's crucial to avoid the common diversification mistakes while choosing an ETF for the long run. Let's explore this along with some other strategies to optimize ETF returns.

Diversify mindfully

Mindful diversification involves not getting influenced by what is popular or what the 'other' investors are doing. Your ETF portfolio needs to reflect your personal investment philosophy, investment goals, and risk tolerance. Two key elements of mindful diversification are: 1. Avoiding the poorly designed indexes that don't fulfill your diversification goals, and 2. Uncovering the underlying risks in an index.

We pretty much covered the first point at the beginning of this chapter. One key takeaway is that broad-index ETFs (for instance, Vanguard Total Stock Market ETF (VTI)), with a substantial number of components and lower concentrations better serve your diversification goals.

Talking about the second point, the 3 main indicators of gauging risks are volatility, drawdown, and concentration. Even though you may have an investment horizon of 10 or 15 years, you wouldn't like your portfolio to go through a turbulent adventure along the way. So, if we compare Invesco QQQ Trust (QQQ) and Vanguard S&P 500 ETF (VOO), QQQ generated much higher historical returns however it experienced more volatility (fluctuations in its price) and steeper drawdowns.

Look at this comparison below:

ETF	10-year annualized returns (Jan 2015 - Oct 2024)	Standard Deviation (a measure of volatility	Max. drawdown
Invesco QQQ Trust (QQQ)	17.9%	18.7%	32.6%
Vanguard S&P 500 ETF (VOO)	12.9%	15.3%	23.9%

Table 3: Comparing QQQ and VOO

> **The bottom line**: While index ETFs like VOO may look less flashy, they are more effective in managing risks (and ensuring a good night's sleep).

Know the tax implications

Broadly speaking, ETFs are much more tax-efficient compared to mutual funds. When mutual funds, especially the actively managed ones, repeatedly buy and sell their holdings for rebalancing, any resulting gains need to be distributed to investors. These frequent capital gain distributions create taxable events for investors.

However, index-based equity ETFs are much more tax-efficient mainly because they tend not to distribute a lot of capital gains. This is because these ETFs passively track an index and they rebalance their holdings only when the index changes its constituent stocks. Moreover, ETFs' unique creation and redemption mechanism (discussed in Chapter 2) and their tradability in the secondary market lower their turnover and capital gains distribution.

The following figure (based on Data from the inception of each fund to 12/31/23) shows that irrespective of active or passive investing style, a minuscule of equity ETFs distributed capital gains compared to equity mutual funds:

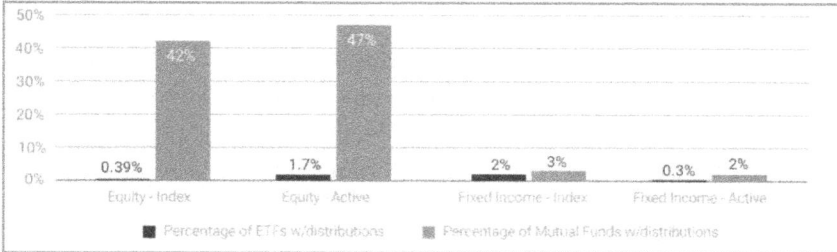

Figure 21: *Funds with distributions (%). (Source: americancentury.com)*

Moreover, low turnover by ETFs ensures that a greater share of the gains qualifies for long-term capital gains (which are taxed at a lower rate than short-term gains). According to BlackRock, the tax costs of the average active U.S. equity mutual fund are more than double the expense ratio.

Short and long-term capital gains taxes

Despite several tax advantages of ETFs, remember that you are liable to pay taxes on any dividend income, capital gains distribution, or interest income (in the case of fixed-income ETFs). Moreover, when you sell an equity or bond ETF, your tax liability depends on the duration of your holding. In case the holding period exceeds 1 year, long-term capital gains taxes apply (at a rate up to 23.8% in the US, including the 3.8% Net Investment Income Tax (NIIT)). However, for holding periods lower than a year, you will be taxed at the ordinary income rate (which can go up to 40.8 percent including NIIT). So, holding your ETFs longer can help save on taxes.

However, another important thing to remember is that these tax rates apply when you hold ETFs in a taxable account such as a brokerage account. For ETFs held in tax-deferred accounts (for instance, 401(k) s and traditional IRAs), you generally won't be taxed until you make a withdrawal (in that case, withdrawals are taxed at your current ordinary income tax rate). Some investors prefer to hold ETFs in tax-deferred accounts to defer tax obligations and maximize tax benefits.

Tax-loss harvesting and the wash-sale rule

Tax-loss harvesting can help you manage your tax bills while realizing capital gains from ETFs. In the context of ETFs, tax-loss harvesting is the practice of selling funds that have declined in value to realize a loss and use it to offset capital gains or reduce taxable income.

Let's take an example to understand this.

Imagine you sold an ETF A for a gain of $3,000. This gain would typically increase your taxable income.

Tax-loss harvesting action: Now, suppose you own 100 shares of another ETF called ETF B, purchased at $50 each, and the price has dropped to $30. If you sell the shares, you realize a loss of $2,000 ($20 loss per share × 100 shares).

Result: This $2,000 loss can offset the $3,000 gain from your other investment, reducing your taxable gain to $1,000. This strategy effectively lowers your overall tax liability for the year while allowing you to reinvest in a different ETF to maintain market exposure.

Now you can use the sale proceeds of $2,000 from the losing ETF to invest in another similar ETF to remain invested in the long run. Note that tax-loss harvesting is subject to the wash-sales rule, which disallows tax-loss harvesting if you buy the same security, a contract or option to buy the security, or a "substantially identical" security, within 30 days before or after the date you sold the loss-generating investment.

So, to prevent a wash sale, consider replacing the sold ETF with a different ETF (or multiple ETFs) that holds similar but not identical assets. For example: Selling an S&P 500 ETF t0 to buy one tracking the Russell 1000 Index.

This would help you derive tax benefits at present while staying invested in the market to achieve long-term investment goals. Alternatively, you can wait for the 61-day window to get over to buy the same ETF.

Note that this discussion is only for educational purposes. To devise the best tax strategy for your investments, consider getting in touch with a financial advisor or tax specialist.

Steady steps: the art of dollar-cost averaging

Once you have started investing in ETFs and built your initial portfolio, the next puzzle to solve is how and when to make incremental investments. There is a relatively "boring" way to solve this puzzle and it's called "dollar cost averaging".

Dollar-cost averaging is a strategy where you invest the same amount of money in a specific ETF (or stock or any other asset) at regular intervals (for example, monthly as most people get a monthly paycheck), no matter what the price is at that time. This simple yet powerful technique helps you avoid the temptation or the stress of timing the market while systematically investing your incremental savings.

Dollar-cost averaging also lessens the impact of market ups and downs on your investments. The idea is that when the market goes up, a fixed amount of money buys fewer shares of an ETF and when the market falls, the same amount buys more shares. When you keep repeating this in the long run, it improves your chances of buying an ETF at the best average price with the least effort.

However, you don't have to just take our word for it. Let's check out an example to illustrate why dollar-cost averaging is so effective.

Suppose you started investing $1,000 at the beginning of each month in the SPDR S&P 500 ETF (SPY) starting in 2018 and continued till September 2024. Now, let's look at how the price of SPY has fluctuated over your investing period:

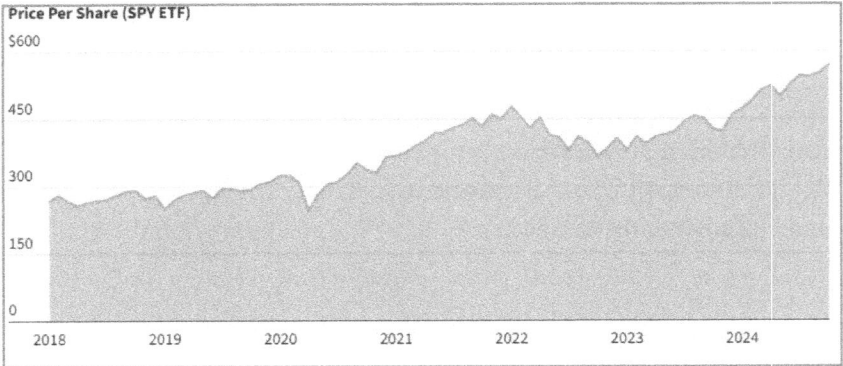

Figure 22: *Fluctuation in the Price of SPY (Source: investopedia.com)*

With changes in the price of SPY, the number of shares you can buy also fluctuates. Since the price has generally shown an upward trend, the number of shares bought each month goes down, as shown in the figure below:

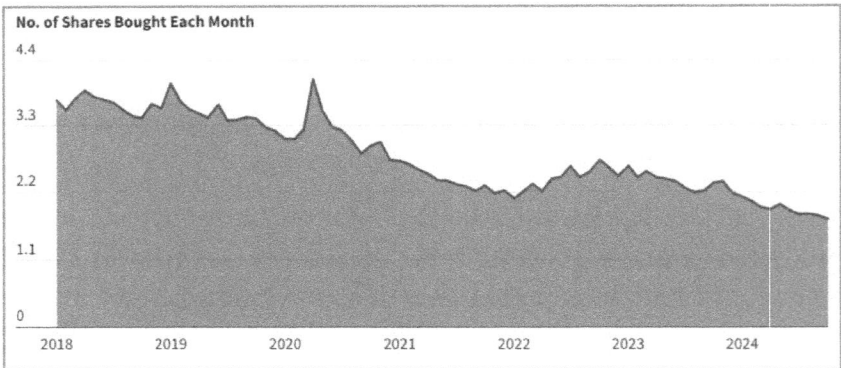

Figure 23: *Units of SPY shares bought each month (Source: investopedia.com)*

Now, let's look at the outcome. This last figure shows the magic of the disciplined approach of dollar-cost averaging in which our total investments of $81,000 ($1,000 * 81 months) turn into $128,000:

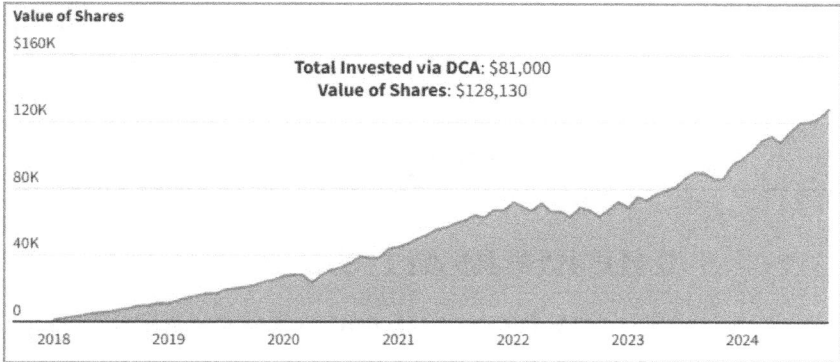

Value of Shares

Total Invested via DCA: $81,000
Value of Shares: $128,130

Figure 24: A steady rise in investment value. (Source: investopedia.com).

Dollar-cost averaging, as shown in the example, gives a laid-back system for investing minus the pain of continuous market monitoring.

Wrapping it up

When it comes to ETF investing (or investing in any asset, for that matter), it's clear that the small details matter. From understanding the limitations of popular indexes like the Dow to the importance of mindful diversification, every choice you make can significantly impact your investment returns. By adopting strategies like dollar-cost averaging and being aware of tax implications, you can navigate the ETF landscape with confidence.

As we have said umpteen times in the book, investing isn't a sprint; it's a marathon. So, take your time and make informed decisions along the way. **There is no hurry. We shall get there someday.**

Chapter 9

THE ETF REALITY CHECK:

MISCONCEPTIONS AND MISTAKES

*"One of the oldest sayings on Wall Street is "Let your winners run,
and cut your losers." It's easy to make a mistake and do the opposite,
pulling out the flowers and watering the weeds."*
- Peter Lynch.

Turducken is a creative dish in which a deboned chicken is stuffed inside a deboned duck, which is then stuffed inside a deboned turkey. Critics often describe ETFs as a turducken. The analogy goes like this: some ETFs have layered complexities hidden inside them. John Bogle, one of the earliest proponents of index funds and passive investing, was not a great fan of ETFs. Bogle even rejected the proposal of listing the first ETF in the US. His view was that the tradability of these instruments would turn them into a losing game for investors and a winning one for brokers. In a paper named *The Dark Side of ETFs*, researchers from the University of Technology Sydney (UTS) found something that can discredit everything written in this book: Data from one of the largest brokerages in Germany shows ETF portfolios underperformed non-ETF portfolios by 2.3% a year.

You would be, however, entirely misled without looking at the caveats. Some ETFs (for instance, leveraged or inverse ones) may be similar to a turducken, but you don't have any compulsion to invest in them. As long as there are speculators under the hood of long-term investors, there will be complex ETFs to serve them (Different strokes for different folks, as they say). Just like we can't blame Coca-Cola

for selling empty calories as long they don't force us to buy them, we can't blame ETF sponsors for adding layers of complexities as long as there are takers. For passive investors, however, there are hundreds of plain-vanilla ETFs meeting all your investing needs.

Plus, you can avoid Bogle's early apprehensions simply by avoiding frequent trading. Just because ETFs are easier to trade doesn't mean you have to churn out your portfolio wearing a day trader's cap.

Bogle said:

> *"...But let me be clear. There is nothing wrong with investing in those indexed ETFs that track the broad stock market, just as long as you don't trade them."*

Moreover, ETF's underperformance, as indicated by the UTS study, happens only when you try to time the market. The same study says, ETF-based portfolios actually outperformed if the investor bought the investment and held it for the long term. The study concludes, "Therefore, adopting a buy-and-hold strategy is more important than selecting better ETFs."

There are 3 key takeaways from this discussion (and, broadly speaking, from this entire book): 1. Avoid what is risky, 2. Stick to broader and simpler ETFs, and 3. Don't try to time the market. This chapter explores some of the key misconceptions and ETF investing mistakes that lead to sub-optimal investment results.

Let's dive in.

Debunking common ETF myths

An ETF myth is a commonly-held misconception that can prevent informed decisions. By debunking these myths, you can unlock greater benefits and make more strategic investment choices. Here are some of the most notable ETF myths and the truths behind them.

Myth 1: ETFs offer only broad market exposure

Truth: While ETFs were originally conceived as index-investing tools to offer broader market exposure, now we have hundreds of ETFs focused on smaller market segments, specific industries, and themes. There are even ETFs tracking a single stock. One example is Direxion Daily TSLA Bull 2X Shares (TSLL) which tracks the daily performance of a single stock: Tesla.

Myth 2: ETFs are all low-cost

Truth: ETFs are supposed to be low-cost investing tools, but there are many exceptions. So, while the Vanguard S&P 500 ETF (VOO) has an expense ratio of 0.03%, the AdvisorShares Ranger Equity Bear ETF (HDGE), an inverse ETF, has an expense ratio of 3.45% (that is 115 times the expense ratio of VOO). In general, broader and passive ETFs have a lower expense ratio compared to their active and narrowly focused counterparts.

Myth 3: All ETFs are based on passive strategies

Truth: To begin with, passive investing was one of the key drivers of ETFs. However, according to Morningstar data, as of September 2024, there are 1,619 active ETFs in the US compared to 2,149 index ETFs.

Myth 4: Active ETFs never outperform passive ETFs

Truth: In investing, there is no gospel truth. Any investment strategy can outperform another strategy in a given period or under special circumstances. So, when we look at a specific time frame, many active ETFs have actually outperformed passively ones (and the opposite is true as well). However, passive ones are more suitable for the long-term goals (such as retirement planning) of most everyday investors (who don't want to spend hours analyzing the market).

Myth 5: An ETF's trading volume is the only indicator of its liquidity

Truth: Because of ETFs' unique creation and redemption mechanism (discussed in Chapter 2), the trading volume of an ETF doesn't give a complete picture of its liquidity. An ETF's liquidity heavily depends on the liquidity of its underlying assets. For instance, equity ETFs in which the underlying stocks are heavily traded have higher liquidity. So, while gauging the liquidity of an ETF, look at the liquidity of its underlying stocks.

Myth 6: ETFs don't generate regular income

Truth: ETFs having dividend-paying stocks or fixed-income ETFs generate regular income. This is why ETFs are getting increasingly popular with passive investors.

A few words about investing mistakes and learning from them

In 1986, Charlie Munger was invited to deliver a commencement speech at Harvard. The speech had a quirky title: *How to Guarantee a Life of Misery.* Munger's first suggestion to lead a miserable life was:

> "First, be unreliable. Do not faithfully do what you have engaged to do. If you will only master this one habit you will more than counterbalance the combined effect of all your virtues, howsoever great."

Drawing a parallel with ETF investing, the best way to ruin your investment results is by being unreliable, unsystematic, and inconsistent with what you have engaged to do. From cashing out at the first sign of volatility to chasing headlines, even many "long-term investors" commit several investing mistakes. Let's look at some common ones.

Mistake 1 - Jumping on the bandwagon: The risk of buying high and selling low:

Market movements are never predictable and it often happens that a breakout is followed by a temporary pullback. So, when you chase a new high or follow the crowd, you end up entering at a high price and getting nervous when the pullback happens. This is a reason new investors frequently end up buying high and selling low. Instead, adopt a disciplined approach or system—such as dollar-cost averaging—rather than trying to chase the market or time your entry points.

Mistake 2 - Panic selling: cashing out when markets get volatile

From January 2004 through January 2024, the S&P 500 has generated an annualized return of 9.8% (turning an investment of $10,000 into $64,870). However, had you missed the best 10 days, the annualized return would be just 5.6% (turning the same $10,000 into $29,735). And, had you missed the best 30 days in these 20 years, you would end up gaining just $1,727 as your initial $10,000 would turn into just $11,727.

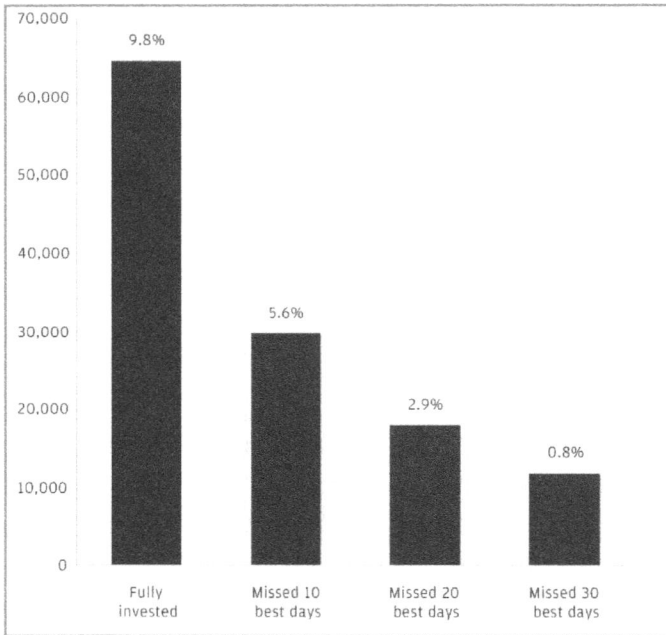

Figure 25: *Performance of the S&P 500: missing the best days (Source: J.P. Morgan Asset Management)*

Additionally, according to JP Morgan's data, between 1980 and 2024, the S&P 500 suffered an average intra-year drawdown of 15%. The index experienced even steeper intra-year losses in 16 of the 44 years. Despite these steep drawdowns, full-year returns were positive in 33 years (75% of the time).

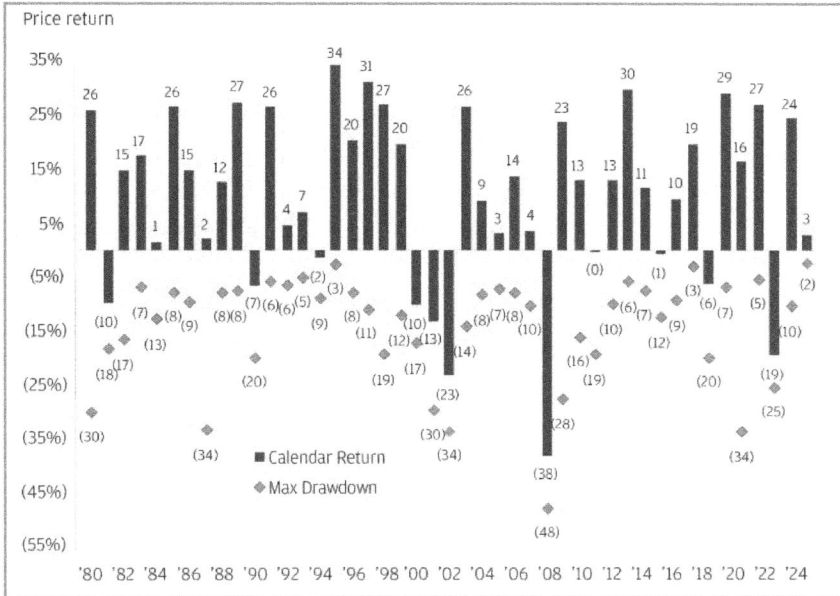

Figure 26: *S&P 500 intra-year declines (max drawdowns) & calendar year price returns* (**Source**: *J.P. Morgan Asset Management*)

> **The bottom line**: Keep investing and stay invested even when the going gets tough. ETF investing is a long-term game.

Mistake 3 - Too little or too much diversification: Diversification helps in managing risks, however, be careful of too little or too much diversification. When you are not diversified enough, your portfolio's performance relies on a handful of stocks or sectors. However, when you are spread too thin across sectors and geographies or have too many ETFs in your portfolio, you run the risk of over-diversification. In Chapter 4, we discussed some of the standardized approaches to building a diversified portfolio.

Mistake 4 - Buying stocks you don't fully understand: Legendary fund manager Peter Lynch said, "Know what you own and know why you own it." ETFs, just like a turducken, may have hidden surprises (in this case, investment risks) because of their holdings, sectoral exposure, or leverage. You must look at the fine print well before investing in

89

one. A simple rule of thumb: Don't buy an ETF if you don't understand where the returns are coming from.

Mistake 5 - Ignoring the small costs: Don't ignore the few basis point differences in the expense ratios of otherwise similar ETFs. For example, there is hardly any practical difference between SPDR S&P 500 ETF Trust (SPY) and Vanguard S&P 500 ETF (VOO), except that SPY has a slightly higher expense ratio (0.09% vs. 0.03%). So, if you are a long-term investor with a multi-decade investing horizon, VOO probably makes more sense given the slightly lower costs.

Wrapping it up

In his 1986 Harvard commencement speech, Munger had another piece of advice to make our lives miserable. He said:

> *"My second prescription for misery is to learn everything you possibly can from your own personal experience, minimizing what you learn vicariously from the good and bad experiences of others, living and dead."*

Making all the mistakes firsthand and trying to learn only from your own experience is a sure-shot way to financial misery. Some errors can be quite costly, taking years to recover from. To avoid that path, we can always learn from the mistakes of others. And, looking around, you'll find no shortage of people making investing mistakes from which you can learn a great deal.

Chapter 10

THE LONG GAME OF ETF INVESTING

"It's amazing how a little tomorrow can make up
for a whole lot of yesterday."
*- **John Guare**, Landscape of the Body.*

In human psychology, *Cognitive Dissonance* is described as a psychological state in which a person's beliefs, values, or attitudes don't align with their actions or with each other. As we were researching this last chapter in the book, a news headline on CNBC caught our attention. It reads: "Here's how much Americans say they need to retire—and it's 53% higher than four years ago." As we explored further, we got to know that a typical American worker believes that they need at least $1.46 million, an all-time high amount, to retire comfortably.

These numbers were pegged at around $951,000 in 2020. The pandemic (along with a long spell of inflation) has likely pushed people to reevaluate their financial needs. According to Aditi Javeri Gokhale, the Chief Strategy Officer at Northwestern Mutual:

"The magic number is at an all-time high — it's 50% higher than
what it was before the pandemic. The cost of living in general,
whether in reality or perception, seems to be more costly now than it
was before."

The problem, however, is that while the average American recognizes the need for higher savings, this awareness has not led to tangible action; in fact, many are saving even less than before. The average retirement savings of US adults have dropped to $88,400 in 2024 from $98,800 in 2021. This means there is now a gap of about $1.37 million between how much an Average American thinks they need for retirement and how much they have actually saved. According to a 2023 survey by financial services firm Credit Karma, about 27% of Americans aged 59 and above have no retirement savings at all.

That's a serious case of cognitive dissonance!

Most people recognize the importance of saving. What they fail to do is to create a habit of saving through a systematic approach. Formation of any new habit must start small, stay consistent, follow a system, and repeatedly do the boring stuff. Fortunately, ETFs can fulfill all the four criteria.

In this chapter, we'll explore how ETFs can pave the way to financial freedom and even make early retirement a reality for you. We'll also discuss emerging trends in the ETF landscape that can help you set realistic expectations for your investment journey.

Let's explore.

Patience pays off: achieving financial freedom through ETF investing

The popular Chinese proverb says, "A journey of a thousand miles begins with a single step". The first step in achieving financial freedom is having a realistic financial goal. A practical financial goal, however, is not a random number to be achieved at a certain time in the future. It needs to be specific and time-bound (for instance, accumulating $1 million in 25 years). Moreover, you need to calculate it based on factors like your age, your future earnings expectations, when you plan to retire, your expected post-retirement expenses, and other financial goals (for instance, buying a house or planning a family).

One simple way to calculate your retirement corpus is to multiply your expected annual expenses by the number of years post-retirement. So, if your post-retirement life expectancy is 30 years and you expect to spend $50,000 each year (The U.S. Bureau of Labor Statistics data shows this is how much an American retiree household spends around in a year) you need a total retirement savings of $1.5 million.

Now, considering the long-term annualized return of the S&P 500 being in the neighborhood of 10%, let's look at the monthly savings required to achieve this goal:

Age at which you start investing	Years remaining until retirement	Required monthly investment
30	35	$1,051
35	30	$1,271
40	25	$1,652
50	15	$3,594

Table 4: *Monthly savings needed at different ages for the $1 million goal*

Investing in broader-market ETFs, like the S&P 500 ETFs, can help you achieve your goals over the long run. However, as the table above shows, the earlier you start, the less you need to invest each month (which results in lower strain on your monthly budget) to achieve the same goal. When the number of years to retire falls by half (from 30 to 15), the required monthly savings go up about 3 fold (from $1,271 to $3,594).

> **The bottom line**: Begin as early as possible and stay committed to your systematic investment plan to let your investments multiply over the years.

As we draw closer to the end of the book, let's explore some emerging themes in ETF investing that can help you make informed decisions.

Future trends in ETF investing

In the 2007 sci-fi action thriller Next, Cris Johnson, the lead character played by Nicolas Cage, made a rather philosophical observation:

"Here is the thing about the future. Every time you look at it, it changes, because you look at it, and that changes everything else".

In the absence of a crystal ball, our next best shot at predicting the future is by looking at the emerging trends at present and extrapolating them into the future. Here are some of these emerging trends in the ETF space:

Trend 1: ETFs' uninhibited growth to continue

Despite ETFs' extraordinary growth in recent years, there is still substantial headroom for further development. According to State Street's 2024 ETF Impact Survey, at present global ETF assets account for less than 12% of investable assets globally. According to the same survey, 63% of US investors plan to buy ETFs in the next 12 months, up from 37% in Q4 2022. Moreover, ETFs are increasingly gaining popularity, reflecting a strong upward trend.

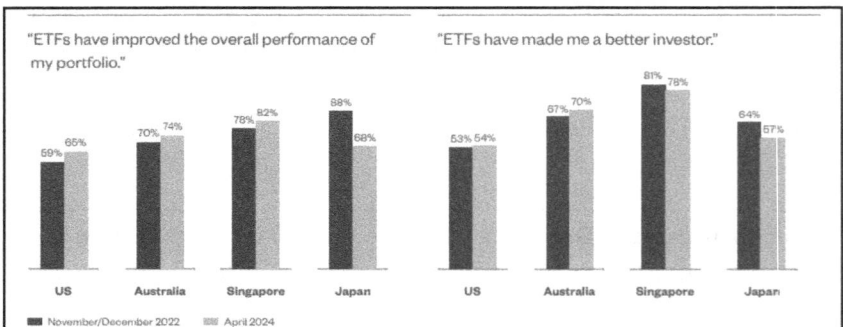

Figure 27: ETFs continue to get high marks from individual investors (Source: State Street Global Advisors, 2024 ETF Impact Survey)

The State Street 2024 ETF Impact Survey also projects the following growth areas in ETFs through 2025:

Growth in number and use of active ETFs	28%
Continued flows out of mutual funds into ETFs	26%
Increased flows into Tech sector ETFs due to interest in AI	26%
Growth in number and use of fixed income ETFs	25%
Growth in number and use of alternatives ETFs	25%
Growth in number and use of dividend ETFs	24%
Growth in number and use of low-cost ETFs	24%
Renewed interest in cryptocurrency due to crypto ETFs	23%
Growth in number and use of ESG/sustainability ETFs	21%
Increased flows into defensive sectors, given the heightened geopolitical risks	20%
Increase in availability and use of ETFs outside of the US	19%

Figure 28: ETF trends that will have the most significant impact on the ETF industry through 2025 (Source: State Street Global Advisors, 2024 ETF Impact Survey)

Trend 2: Active ETFs are growing too

The AUM share of active funds in worldwide ETFs has steadily risen from 0.3% during 2008-2009 to more than 6.4% today. 2023 was a record year in terms of active ETF inflows, in which 20.3% of global ETF inflows, or more than US$160 billion went into active ETFs. Despite the historical evidence in favor of passive investing, ETF sponsors are likely to launch more active funds as long as investors are willing to assume greater risks to beat the market.

Trend 3: More mutual funds are converting to ETFs

In 2023, 35 US mutual funds were converted into ETFs. According to a PWC survey, in the US almost 1 in 4 managers plan to convert at least one mutual fund into an ETF, to attract more investment the increasing popularity of ETFs. The same trends are reflected globally too: 1 in 5 fund managers plan to convert a portion of their mutual fund offerings into ETFs over the next two years.

Trend 4: Young investors are flocking to ETFs

Due to the ease of access and rising popularity, young investors are showing an increased preference for ETFs over mutual funds. Surveys across countries show millennials are showing a greater preference for ETFs over Gen X and Boomers.

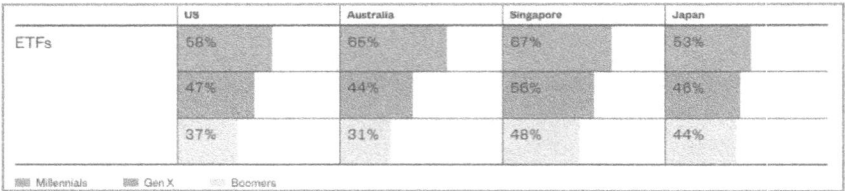

	US	Australia	Singapore	Japan
ETFs	58%	65%	67%	53%
	47%	44%	56%	46%
	37%	31%	48%	44%

Millennials   Gen X   Boomers

Figure 29: Percentage of surveyed investors with ETFs in their current portfolio (Source: State Street Global Advisors, 2024 ETF Impact Survey)

Trend 5: A growing globalization of ETFs

In 2023, European ETFs witnessed an inflow of US$158.2 billion, bringing their total AUM to US$1.8 trillion. 60% of respondents surveyed by State Street Global Advisors expect European ETF AUM to exceed $3 trillion by 2028. Moreover, ETFs from Asia Pacific too are experiencing growing interest from retail investors to fulfill their diversification needs. 77% of survey respondents expect Asia Pacific ETF AUM to reach $2.5 trillion by June 2028.

Combined, all these trends point towards massive expansion in ETF investing in the coming years.

Wrapping it up

In one of the films from the *Pirates of the Caribbean* franchise, the eccentric pirate "Captain" Jack Sparrow says, "Did everyone see that? Because I will not be doing it again." This is exactly how the market often behaves. Just like history, the investing market rarely repeats itself in the same way. New trends, themes, investment philosophies, and instruments are always emerging. The good thing is that despite these changes, many investment fundamentals remain the same. Winning through the long game of ETF investing is probably one of them.

Conclusion

BUILDING A FUTURE WITH ETFS

At the start of this book, we explored how ETFs, and the broader trend of passive investing, have transformed the investing landscape by giving more people a simpler way to build wealth. Fast forward to today, and we're seeing a similar, seismic shift: the growing popularity of ETFs has opened up access to an efficient, low-cost, and resilient investment tool that levels the playing field for individual investors.

As you look to the future, remember that while the investing world is constantly changing, the core principles of successful ETF investing remain consistent. Fads will come and go, market excitement will rise and fall, but ETFs offer a steady path to financial independence without the need to chase the latest trend. Just as we've discussed, the strength of an ETF portfolio lies in its simplicity and diversification, making it the antidote to speculation and "fear of missing out."

Throughout this book, we've focused on teaching you how to apply a disciplined, diversified, and low-cost approach to build your portfolio. We've discussed selecting the right ETFs, understanding their structure, and managing your investments over time. You're now equipped to make informed decisions, keeping your focus on long-term growth while filtering out the noise of the market.

If you take away one golden rule from this book, let it be this: *Invest in what you understand.* Stick to what's simple, clear, and designed to meet your goals. This rule will not only protect your investments but also help you avoid the most common pitfalls that derail even the savviest investors.

I hope this book has given you both the knowledge and the confidence to get started with ETFs and to sustain a consistent path toward financial security. But if there's anything you need more clarity on, or if you'd like personalized guidance, don't hesitate to reach out.

My team and I are here to support you every step of the way. You can contact us at admin@freemanpublications.com, and we'll do our best to help with any questions you may have.

You can also subscribe to our YouTube channel for bi-weekly market updated and insights by going to freemanpublications.com/youtube

If this book has provided value to you, we'd be incredibly grateful if you could leave a review on Amazon. Your feedback shapes our future projects and allows us to better serve readers like you. You can leave a review by visiting freemanpublications.com/leaveareview.

To your future wealth and success,

Oliver El-Gorr

And here's a bonus for you!

This book explains how ETFs can help you build wealth over time through disciplined investing. But what if you could supercharge those returns? If you're ready to leverage your ETFs for extra gains—boosting your earning potential to 15-20%—using smart, low-risk options strategies, then keep reading!

TAKING YOUR ETF INCOME TO THE NEXT LEVEL WITH THE OPTIONS WHEEL STRATEGY

Investing in broad-market ETFs like the SPDR S&P 500 ETF (SPY), Vanguard S&P 500 ETF (VOO), or iShares Core S&P 500 ETF (IVV) allows you to tap into the market's long-term growth potential, historically around 9-10%. This strategy can help you grow your wealth steadily over time. Now if you combine ETF investing with a low-risk options strategy called options wheel, you can potentially double this return.

Broadly speaking, the options wheel strategy involves cyclically selling cash-secured puts and covered calls to earn regular income on any optionable instrument like stock or ETFs. The wheel strategy initially started with the basic idea of a covered call (in which you sell call options on a stock that you already own). In the options wheel strategy, we start with selling cash-secured put options. In the second part of the cycle, we move to selling covered calls.

This strategy has become popular with regular investors because of its straightforwardness and the potential to generate income from the premiums earned by selling options. Unlike many other types of options trading, the wheel strategy is much safer. It helps make money from the premiums while also giving you chances to buy or sell stocks in a planned way.

Don't worry if you are not familiar with options. Let's break down the options wheel strategy into its most basic form. But, before that let's get acquitted with some of the key terminologies.

Options wheel: key terminologies

These are some of the key terminologies related to the options wheel strategy:

1. **Cash-secured puts**: A put option sold with enough cash set aside to buy the underlying stock or ETF, if assigned.

2. **Assignment**: The event when an option seller has to fulfill their obligation to buy or sell the underlying ETF, usually when the option is exercised by the buyer.

3. **Covered calls**: A strategy where an investor sells call options on shares they already own, generating income from premiums while potentially capping future profits.

4. **Premium**: The price paid for an option, which is received by the option seller when selling puts or calls.

5. **Strike price**: The price at which the underlying asset can be bought or sold when the option is exercised.

6. **Expiration date**: The date on which an option contract becomes invalid and the right to exercise it no longer exists.

These terms are essential for understanding and executing the Wheel strategy effectively.

Now, let's get deeper into the options wheel strategy with examples.

Simplifying the options wheel strategy

The options wheel strategy has these 3 broad steps:

Step 1: Sell cash-secured puts on an ETF until the option is exercised and you are assigned the ETF shares (typically, 100 shares of an ETF for every put sold).

Step 2: Once you have the shares, sell covered calls on that ETF until the option gets exercised again and your shares are sold.

Step 3: Keep repeating this process!

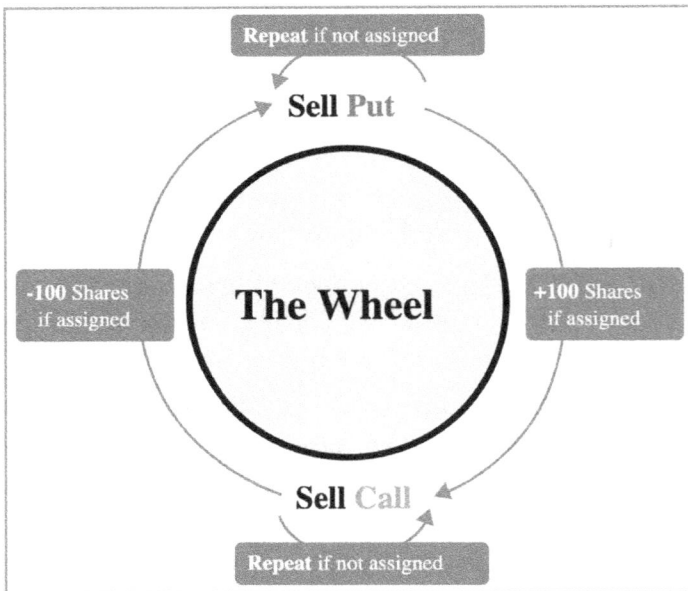

The options wheel strategy (Source: *optionstrat.com*)

Let's expand these steps using an example:

Step 1: Sell cash-secured puts:

◇ Here, we will first choose an ETF you believe will perform well in the long term and you want it to be part of your portfolio. Let's say the ETF is currently trading at $75.

◇ Let's now sell cash-secured puts at a strike price where you wouldn't mind owning the ETF. For instance, you sell the $65 puts for a premium of $3.

◇ This means you are willing to buy the ETF at $65 per share if the price falls below that level. If the ETF remains above $65 at expiration, you keep the premium ($300 per contract) and can continue selling puts after each expiry and keep pocketing the premiums. You can continue selling these puts until one expires in the money (the ETF's price is below the strike price at expiration), at which point the shares will be assigned to you.

If the assignment happens:

◇ If the ETF closes below the $65 strike price at expiration, you will be assigned 100 shares at $65 for each put option you sold.

◇ You effectively purchased the ETF at a discount (your break-even price is $62 after accounting for the premium received).

STEP 2: Sell covered calls:

◇ Now that you own the ETF shares, you can sell covered calls. Choose an out-of-the-money call option to sell, such as the $85 calls, which, let's assume, are trading for $2 each.

◇ If the ETF stays below $85 at expiration, you keep the premium and can repeatedly sell more calls.

If the assignment happens:

⋄ If the ETF rises above $85, your shares will be called away, meaning you sell your shares at that price. You will also keep the $200 premium from selling the call and any capital gains from the difference between your purchase price ($65) and the selling price ($85).

⋄ If your shares are called away, you can restart the process by selling puts again and moving to step 1.

STEP 3: Repeat the process:

⋄ Whether you keep your ETF shares or they are called away, you can continue the cycle of selling cash-secured puts and covered calls, creating a steady stream of income while managing your investment.

The main way to make money with the Wheel strategy is by collecting the premiums from selling puts and calls on the ETF. Every time you sell these options, you earn money, which can add up over time. You can also make additional profits if you sell the ETF for more than what you paid for it. **So, you have two potential sources of income: the premiums from options and any capital gains from selling the ETF at a higher price.**

To implement the options wheel strategy, find a highly liquid ETF (for instance, SPY or VOO) that you're confident in and are willing to hold for the long term. Once you pick an ETF you like, sell out-of-the-money puts at a price where you wouldn't mind owning it. Keep selling puts to collect more premiums until you're assigned shares at your chosen strike price.

After you own the ETF shares, start selling calls against them until the call options are exercised. When that happens, your ETF will be sold, locking in any gains along with the premiums you collected.

Indicative Returns Using the
Options Wheel Strategy on SPY

Here's an example of potential returns based on on specific assumptions:

Step 1: Sell cash-secured puts

◇ Current price: $598

◇ Sell an out-of-the-money put option at a $590 strike price for a premium of $4.33 per share.

◇ If assigned, you would purchase 100 shares at $590, totaling $59,000. Your break-even would be $585.67 after accounting for the premium collected.

If SPY remains above $590, you keep the $433 premium.

Step 2: Assigned shares - sell covered calls

Now that you own 100 shares of SPY at $590, sell a covered call at the $610 strike price for a premium of $3.48 per share.

◇ If SPY rises above $610, your shares will be called away, and you'll sell them for $61,000.

◇ Your total profit will be $2,000 (from selling the shares) + $348 (from the call premium) = $2,348.

◇ If SPY stays below $610, you retain the $348 premium and can sell another call option.

Annualized return calculation

Assuming you repeat this process 12 times a year (6 times for puts and 6 times for calls), your potential income could be around:

◇ **Puts:** $433 x 6 = $2,598

◇ **Calls:** $348 x 6 = $2,088

◇ **Total Annual Income:** $2,598 + $2,088 = $4,686

With an initial investment of $59,000, this results in an annualized return of approximately 7.95%.

Now, if we assume a dividend yield of 1.2% on SPY ETFs, your total return with the options wheel strategy would be higher than 9%.

Here are some projected income totals using current market data for different ETFs:

ETF	Annualized Income from Options (30 Delta)	Dividend Yield	Total Annualized Income
SCHD (U.S. Dividend Equity)	12%	3.50%	15.50%
GLD (Gold ETF)	13%	0%	13%
IYR (U.S. Real Estate)	14.20%	2.56%	16.76%
IWM (Russell 2000)	18.80%	1.18%	19.98%
QQQ (Nasdaq-100)	19%	0.46%	19.46%

SMH (Semiconductors)	33%	0.42%	33.42%

How the options wheel strategy benefits you

You can derive several benefits from the options wheel strategy using ETFs irrespective of whether you are a trader or a long-term investor:

◇ **Consistent income:** By selling puts and calls, you generate regular income from the premiums you collect. This can provide a steady cash flow, which is especially useful for covering expenses or reinvesting.

◇ **Potential to buy ETFs at a discount:** When you sell cash-secured puts, you have the chance to buy the ETF at a lower price. If the market price drops below the strike price of your puts, you get assigned shares at that price, often below what you would have paid otherwise.

◇ **Capital gains opportunities:** Once you own the ETF shares, you can sell covered calls. If the ETF price rises above your call strike price, your shares will be sold for a profit. This means you not only earn the premium from selling the call but also gain from the increase in the ETF's price.

◇ **Flexibility and control:** The wheel strategy allows you to choose a strike prices and expiration dates that fit your investment goals. You can adjust your strategy based on market conditions, your risk tolerance, and how long you want to hold the ETF.

Overall, the options wheel strategy provides a systematic approach for generating income, buying at discounts, and realizing capital gains. This makes it a great option for long-term investors looking to achieve financial freedom while managing risks.

If you want to learn more about how the wheel strategy works, check out our book, *The Options Wheel Strategy*, available on Amazon.

Join the ranks of savvy investors today!

GLOSSARY

◇ **Active Fund Management:** A strategy where fund managers select stocks to outperform a benchmark index.

◇ **Active ETFs:** ETFs that aim to beat the market by actively choosing its component assets rather than benchmarking a broad index.

◇ **Passive ETFs:** ETFs designed to replicate market indices, typically at lower costs.

◇ **All-Weather Portfolio:** A diversified investment strategy designed to perform well under various economic conditions.

◇ **Assets Under Management (AUM):** The total market value of assets managed on behalf of clients.

◇ **Authorized Participant (AP):** A financial institution that can create and redeem ETF shares.

◇ **Black Monday:** October 19, 1987, marked by the largest one-day stock market crash in U.S. history.

◇ **Bond ETFs:** Funds holding diversified portfolios of bonds traded on exchanges.

◇ **Brokerage Account:** An account for buying and selling securities through a broker.

◇ **Calendar-Based Rebalancing:** Regular portfolio rebalancing at set intervals, regardless of market conditions.

◇ **Circuit Breakers:** Mechanisms to halt trading during significant market declines.

◇ **Cognitive Dissonance:** The mental state of holding conflicting beliefs and actions.

◇ **Compound Annual Growth Rate (CAGR):** The annual rate at which an investment would grow if it increased in value at the same rate each year from its initial to final value.

◇ **Concentration Risk:** Risk from heavy investment in a few assets, increasing volatility.

◇ **Core-Satellite Strategy:** A stable core portfolio combined with higher-risk investments.

◇ **Diversification:** The technique of spreading investments across assets to reduce risk.

◇ **Dollar-Cost Averaging:** Investing a fixed amount regularly, regardless of price.

◇ **Dow Jones Industrial Average (DJIA):** One of the most popular and widely recognized stock market indices measuring the daily stock market movements of 30 U.S. publicly traded companies.

◇ **Efficient Market Hypothesis (EMH):** Theory stating stock prices reflect all available information.

◇ **Equity ETFs:** ETFs that primarily invest in stocks.

◇ **ETFs (Exchange-Traded Funds):** Funds traded on exchanges, allowing diversified investment in one transaction.

◇ **Expense Ratio:** The annual fee for managing an ETF, expressed as a percentage of assets.

◇ **Index ETFs:** ETFs that track specific market indices.

◇ **Inverse ETFs:** ETFs that aim to deliver returns that are the opposite of the performance of a specific underlying index, allowing investors to profit from declines in that index.

◇ **Investment Fundamentals:** Core principles for successful investing, like diversification and long-term planning.

◇ **Leveraged ETFs:** ETFs that amplify returns through derivatives and debt.

◇ **Liquidity:** Ease of buying or selling an asset without affecting its price.

◇ **Market Capitalization:** Total market value of a company's outstanding shares.

◇ **Market Volatility:** Variation in asset prices over time.

◇ **Millennial Investors:** Individuals typically aged 25 to 40 who favor cost-effective ETFs due to their accessibility, lower fees, and potential for higher returns.

◇ **Myopic Loss Aversion:** Over-sensitivity to short-term losses affecting long-term decisions.

◇ **Negative Correlation:** When one asset's value increases as another decreases.

◇ **Net Asset Value (NAV):** Value of an investment fund's assets minus liabilities.

◇ **Niche ETFs:** Specialized ETFs targeting specific sectors or themes.

◇ **Passive Investing:** Strategy aiming to match market returns with minimal trading.

◇ **Portfolio Rebalancing:** Realigning asset proportions to maintain desired risk.

◇ **Price-Weighted Index:** An index weighted by stock price rather than market capitalization.

◇ **Random Walk Theory:** A theory suggesting that stock price movements are random and unpredictable.

◇ **Robo-Advisors:** Automated platforms managing investment portfolios at lower costs.

◇ **Small-Cap ETFs:** ETFs focusing on small-cap companies seeking high growth.

◇ **SPIVA Report (S&P Indices Versus Active):** Compares active fund performance against benchmarks.

◇ **Superstock:** Stocks that generate significant returns and contribute to market wealth.

◇ **Tax Efficiency:** Ability to minimize tax liabilities through strategic investment choices.

◇ **Tax-Loss Harvesting:** Selling losing investments to offset gains and reduce tax liabilities.

◇ **Thematic ETFs:** ETFs targeting specific investment themes or trends.

◇ **Threshold-Based Rebalancing:** Adjustments made when an asset's allocation exceeds set limits.

◇ **Transparency:** The extent to which an ETF discloses its holdings and strategies.

Why I Started Freeman Publications

My introduction to investing was watching my grandfather lose almost everything in the 2008 crash. Despite being a war hero, multi-lingual and a successful businessman - he fell foul of bad advice and saw his portfolio crumble in the Global Financial Crisis. That sparked my lifelong learning journey with the goal of avoiding the mistakes he made.

I found that most investing-focused content spent too much time focusing on the minutia or what I call the spreadsheet-side of investing, and very little on the human element. Thus being fundamentally inaccessible to the average person.

My goal with these books is to explain financial concepts in plain English, with real examples so that you can apply the information in your own portfolio. That is because I truly believe the average individual investor is better equipped to "beat the market" long term than most Wall Street professionals.

I also wants these books to be something that pass down through multiple generations, since I became a father in 2024, I now think with an even longer time horizon. I hope one day my daughter will be in a better financial position than me, but that all starts with having the right knowledge.

That's why Freeman Publications exists.

Oliver El-Gorr

REFERENCES

Chapter 01

◇ VFINX | Vanguard 500 index fund; investor overview | MarketWatch. Available at: https://www.marketwatch.com/investing/fund/vfinx (Accessed: 05 November 2024).

◇ 10 largest mutual funds by AUM | investing | U.S. news. Available at: https://money.usnews.com/investing/articles/largest-mutual-funds-by-aum (Accessed: 05 November 2024).

◇ It's official: Passive Funds Overtake Active Funds | morningstar. Available at: https://www.morningstar.com/funds/recovery-us-fund-flows-was-weak-2023 (Accessed: 05 November 2024).

◇ Birth of the index mutual fund: 'Bogle's folly' turns 40 - WSJ. Available at: https://www.wsj.com/articles/BL-MBB-52953 (Accessed: 05 November 2024).

◇ The first U.S. Open-end mutual fund, Massachusetts ... Available at: https://www.pionline.com/reporters-notebook/first-us-open-end-mutual-fund-massachusetts-investors-trust-celebrates-its-100th (Accessed: 05 November 2024).

◇ Brown Brothers Harriman (2024) Origins of the Modern Mutual Fund, Brown Brothers Harriman. Available at: https://www.bbh.com/us/en/bbh-who-we-are/our-story/200-years-of-partnership/origins-of-the-modern-mutual-fund.html (Accessed: 05 November 2024).

◇ PricewaterhouseCoopers, ETFS 2028: Shaping the future, PwC. Available at: https://www.pwc.com/gx/en/industries/financial-services/publications/etfs-2028-shaping-the-future.html (Accessed: 05 November 2024).

◇ Bhasin, T. (2023) What is the Bogle index fund strategy? Learn About Investment Tax Saving and Financial Planning. Available at: https://www.etmoney.com/learn/personal-finance/what-is-the-bogle-index-fund-strategy/ (Accessed: 05 November 2024).

Chapter 02

◇ U.S. Persistence scorecard year-end 2023 - Spiva (2024) S&P Dow Jones Indices. Available at: https://www.spglobal.com/spdji/en/spiva/article/us-persistence-scorecard (Accessed: 05 November 2024).

◇ The best stock over the last 30 years? You've never heard of IT - WSJ. Available at: https://www.wsj.com/articles/BL-MBB-45711 (Accessed: 05 November 2024).

◇ Johnson, Dr.R.R. (2017) Needles in a stock Picker's haystack: Can you find the 4%?, HuffPost. Available at: https://www.huffpost.com/entry/needles-in-a-stock-pickers-haystack-can-you-find_b_59568425e4b0326c0a8d0fe0 (Accessed: 05 November 2024).

◇ Mitchell, A.C. (2024) Historical average stock market returns for S&P 500 (5-year to 150-year averages), Trade That Swing. Available at: https://tradethatswing.com/average-historical-stock-market-returns-for-sp-500-5-year-up-to-150-year-averages. (Accessed: 05 November 2024).

◇ How much would $10,000 invested in Apple Stock 20 years ago be worth today? | investing | U.S. news. Available at: https://money.usnews.com/investing/articles/apple-aapl-stock-investment-worth-today (Accessed: 05 November 2024).

◇ Krantz, M. (2024) Investors finally throw in the towel on active fund managers, Investor's Business Daily. Available at: https://www. investors.com/etfs-and-funds/personal-finance/sp500-actively-managed-funds-vs-passive/ (Accessed: 05 November 2024).

◇ Traditional index fund vs. ETF cage match | morningstar. Available at: https://www.morningstar.com/funds/traditional-index-fund-vs-etf-cage-match (Accessed: 05 November 2024).

◇ Finance, W.G., ETF versus Mutual Fund Fees, Fidelity. Available at: https://www.fidelity.com/learning-center/investment-products/ etf/etfs-cost-comparison (Accessed: 05 November 2024).

◇ Do stocks outperform treasury bills? W. P. Carey School of Business at ASU. Available at: https://wpcarey.asu.edu/department-finance/ faculty-research/do-stocks-outperform-treasury-bills (Accessed: 05 November 2024).

◇ Spiva India year-end 2023 - Spiva (2024) S&P Dow Jones Indices. Available at: https://www.spglobal.com/spdji/en/spiva/article/ spiva-india/ (Accessed: 05 November 2024).

◇ Bessembinder, H. (Hank) et al. (2019) 'Do global stocks outperform US Treasury bills?', SSRN Electronic Journal [Preprint]. doi:10.2139/ ssrn.3415739.

Chapter 03

◇ What are the different types of ETFs? | etf.com. Available at: https:// www.etf.com/sections/etf-basics/what-are-different-types-etfs (Accessed: 05 November 2024).

◇ The investor's guide to ETFs: Building Resilient Portfolios. Available at: https://www.ssga.com/library-content/assets/pdf/north-america/etf-education/spdr-investors-guide-to-etfs-brochure.pdf (Accessed: 05 November 2024).

◇ ETFs, born from the 1987 market crash, are so far making 2020 less awful - MarketWatch. Available at: https://www.marketwatch. com/story/etfs-born-from-1987-market-crash-are-so-far-making-2020-less-awful-2020-03-18 (Accessed: 05 November 2024).

◇ Best ETFs for November 2024 - Bankrate. Available at: https://www.bankrate.com/investing/best-etfs/ (Accessed: 05 November 2024).

◇ Black Monday market crash (2024) Corporate Finance Institute. Available at: https://corporatefinanceinstitute.com/resources/equities/black-monday/ (Accessed: 05 November 2024).

◇ Different types of ETFs – ETFs simplified: Ishares, BlackRock. Available at: https://www.blackrock.com/sg/en/ishares/education/types-of-etfs (Accessed: 05 November 2024).

◇ ETFGI reports the global ETFs industry had a record 1,192 new product launches in the first 8 months of the Year (2024) ETFGI LLP. Available at: https://etfgi.com/news/press-releases/2024/09/etfgi-reports-global-etfs-industry-had-record-1192-new-products (Accessed: 05 November 2024).

◇ Finance, W.G., What are commodity ETFs? Fidelity. Available at: https://www.fidelity.com/learning-center/investment-products/etf/types-of-etfs-commodity (Accessed: 05 November 2024).

◇ John L. Jacobs, opinion contributor (2017) ETFs rose from the ashes of Black Monday. now they must innovate., The Hill. Available at: https://thehill.com/opinion/finance/356590-etfs-rose-from-the-ashes-of-black-monday-now-they-must-innovate/ (Accessed: 05 November 2024).

Chapter 04

◇ J. (2024) Stock-bond correlation hits multi-decade high, FS Investments. Available at: https://fsinvestments.com/fs-insights/chart-of-the-week-2024-1-5-stock-bond-correlation/ (Accessed: 05 November 2024).

◇ Bridgewater (2020) The all-weather story, Bridgewater. Available at: https://www.bridgewater.com/research-and-insights/the-all-weather-story (Accessed: 05 November 2024).

◇ Keeffe, H. (2020) Why was the potato so important?, RTE. ie. Available at: https://www.rte.ie/history/the-great-irish-famine/2020/0715/1153525-why-was-the-potato-so-important/ (Accessed: 05 November 2024).

◇ Schwab.com, 3 ways to build an all-ETF portfolio, Schwab Brokerage. Available at: https://www.schwab.com/learn/story/3-ways-to-build-all-etf-portfolio (Accessed: 05 November 2024).

◇ Backtesting for the European index investor. Available at: https://curvo.eu/backtest/en/portfolio/ray-dalio-all-weather (Accessed: 05 November 2024).

Chapter 05

◇ Vanguard Australia Personal Investor. Available at: https://www.vanguard.com.au/personal/learn/smart-investing/etfs/how-to-build-an-etf-portfolio (Accessed: 05 November 2024).

◇ Chappatta, B. et al. (2017) Bloomberg billionaires index, Bloomberg.com. Available at: https://www.bloomberg.com/billionaires/ (Accessed: 05 November 2024).

◇ How many ETFs should you have in your portfolio? Yahoo! Finance. Available at: https://finance.yahoo.com/news/many-etfs-portfolio-173252451.html (Accessed: 05 November 2024).

◇ James Royal, Ph.D. (2024) Best online brokers for ETFs in November 2024, Bankrate. Available at: https://www.bankrate.com/investing/best-online-brokers-for-etfs/ (Accessed: 05 November 2024).

◇ Schwab.com, 3 ways to build an all-ETF portfolio, Schwab Brokerage. Available at: https://www.schwab.com/learn/story/3-ways-to-build-all-etf-portfolio (Accessed: 05 November 2024).

◇ Warren Buffett accumulated 99% of his net worth after turning 50 and didn't become a billionaire until 56: 'The biggest thing about making money is time. You don't have to be particularly smart, you just have to be patient, Yahoo! Finance. Available at: https://finance.yahoo.com/news/warren-buffett-accumulated-99-net-193522940.html (Accessed: 05 November 2024).

Chapter 06

◇ What is ETF rebalancing? Benefits & costs. Available at: https://www.etf.com/sections/etf-basics/what-etf-rebalancing-benefits-costs (Accessed: 05 November 2024).

◇ How rebalancing can help reduce volatility in your portfolio. Available at: https://www.fidelity.com/bin-public/060_www_fidelity_com/documents/PAS_rebalancing-portfolio.pdf (Accessed: 05 November 2024).

◇ Boram Lee et al. (2016) Myopic loss aversion and stock investments: An empirical study of private investors, Journal of Banking & Finance. Available at: https://www.sciencedirect.com/science/article/abs/pii/S0378426616300401. (Accessed: 05 November 2024).

◇ Ben Johnson, C., When markets are tough, don't look, Morningstar MY. Available at: https://my.morningstar.com/my/news/180988/when-markets-are-tough-dont-look.aspx (Accessed: 05 November 2024).

◇ Curvo (2023) Why rebalancing your portfolio of ETFs is Sensible, Curvo. Available at: https://curvo.eu/article/rebalance-portfolio-etf (Accessed: 05 November 2024).

◇ Lazaroff, P. (2024) Myopic loss aversion, Plancorp. Available at: https://www.plancorp.com/blog/myopic-loss-aversion (Accessed: 05 November 2024).

◇ Gravier. E. (2021) Nearly half of investors check their performance at least once a day - here's why that's a problem, CNBC. Available at: https://www.cnbc.com/select/how-often-should-you-check-your-investment-portfolio/ (Accessed: 05 November 2024).

Chapter 07

◇ Blackrock launches three targeted ETFs for investors looking to diversify risks | Reuters. Available at: https://www.reuters.com/business/finance/blackrock-launches-three-targeted-etfs-investors-looking-diversify-risks-2024-10-24/ (Accessed: 05 November 2024).

◇ 35% of the S&P 500 is concentrated in the 'Magnificent Seven.' here's what that means for your portfolio., Nasdaq. Available at: https://www.nasdaq.com/articles/35-sp-500-concentrated-magnificent-seven-heres-what-means-your-portfolio (Accessed: 05 November 2024).

◇ Allan Small, F. (2024) The magnificent 7 versus the other 493 S&P 500 companies: What's The Better Investment?, MoneySense. Available at: https://www.moneysense.ca/save/investing/stocks/the-magnificent-7-vs-the-sp-500-companies/ (Accessed: 05 November 2024).

◇ Arnott, A.C., 15 ETFs that have destroyed the most wealth over the past decade, Morningstar CA. Available at: https://www.morningstar.ca/ca/news/230000/15-etfs-that-have-destroyed-the-most-wealth-over-the-past-decade.aspx (Accessed: 05 November 2024).

◇ Equal weight ETF inflows surge as investors bet on Cyclical Shift (2021) ETF Stream. Available at: https://www.etfstream.com/articles/equal-weight-etf-inflows-surge-as-investors-bet-on-cyclical-shift (Accessed: 05 November 2024).

◇ ETF Central, Available at: https://www.etfcentral.com/news/is-it-time-for-investors-to-consider-equal-weighted-etfs (Accessed: 05 November 2024).

◇ What are ETF risks? Fidelity. Available at: https://www.fidelity.com/learning-center/investment-products/etf/risks-with-etfs (Accessed: 05 November 2024).

◇ Henssler Financial (2022) Leveraged ETFs-buyer beware, Henssler Financial. Available at: https://www.henssler.com/leveraged-etfs-buyer-beware/ (Accessed: 05 November 2024).

◇ Johnson, S. (2023) Secretive active ETFs lose out to their fully transparent rivals, Financial Times. Available at: https://www.ft.com/content/d97920eb-5bd2-4270-a591-fe93baa79ec3 (Accessed: 05 November 2024).

◇ State Street Global Advisors announces changes to US SPDR® ETF lineup (2017) Business Wire. Available at: https://www.businesswire.com/news/home/20170630005064/en/State-Street-Global-Advisors-Announces-Changes-to-US-SPDR%C2%AE-ETF-Lineup (Accessed: 05 November 2024).

Chapter 08

◇ Imperfect indexes – choosing a better index ETF | morningstar. Available at: https://www.morningstar.com/funds/choosing-better-index-etf (Accessed: 05 November 2024).

◇ 3 mistakes to avoid when choosing an ETF | Morningstar. Available at: https://www.morningstar.com/funds/3-etf-investment-mistakes-avoid (Accessed: 05 November 2024).

◇ Beers, B., Dollar-cost averaging with ETFs, Investopedia. Available at: https://www.investopedia.com/articles/mutualfund/05/etfdollarcost.asp (Accessed: 05 November 2024).

◇ Forget the Dow Jones -- buy this magnificent ETF instead, Yahoo! Finance. Available at: https://finance.yahoo.com/news/forget-dow-jones-buy-magnificent-134500556.html (Accessed: 05 November 2024).

◇ The Russell 2000 is flawed - this ETF plays it in a better way for quality, Yahoo! Finance. Available at: https://finance.yahoo.com/news/russell-2000-flawed-etf-plays-144900025.html (Accessed: 05 November 2024).

⬧ Schwab.com, ETFs, and taxes: What you need to know, Schwab Brokerage. Available at: https://www.schwab.com/learn/story/etfs-and-taxes-what-you-need-to-know (Accessed: 05 November 2024).

⬧ Understanding the Tax Efficiency of ETFs (2024) Understanding the Tax Efficiency of ETFs | American Century. Available at: https://www.americancentury.com/insights/understanding-tax-efficiency-etfs/ (Accessed: 05 November 2024).

Chapter 09

⬧ Diversification: How much is too much? Available at: https://etf.macquarie.com/us/en/resources/insights/diversification-how-much-is-too-much.html (Accessed: 05 November 2024).

⬧ S&P 500 investing: When to choose spy & when to choose voo - ETF focuses on TheStreet: ETF research and trade ideas. Available at: https://www.thestreet.com/etffocus/trade-ideas/sp-500-investing-when-to-choose-spy-when-to-choose-voo (Accessed: 05 November 2024).

⬧ Will active ETFs outnumber passive ETFs? | morningstar. Available at: https://www.morningstar.com/funds/will-active-etfs-outnumber-passive-etfs (Accessed: 05 November 2024).

⬧ Bhattacharya, U. et al. (no date) The Dark Side of ETFs and Index Funds [2013]. Available at: https://www.uts.edu.au/sites/default/files/FDG_Seminar_140917.pdf (Accessed: 05 November 2024).

⬧ Morgan Private Bank U.S. Available at: https://privatebank.jpmorgan.com/nam/en/insights/markets-and-investing/the-five-most-popular-investing-mistakes-of-2024 (Accessed: 05 November 2024).

⬧ Jayamanne, S. (2024a) Why ETFs may not be the best choice for investors, Morningstar. Available at: https://www.morningstar.com.au/insights/etfs/237548/why-etfs-may-not-be-the-best-choice-for-investors (Accessed: 05 November 2024).

Chapter 10

◇ Lee, M. (2024) The amount of money Americans think they need to retire comfortably hits record high: Study, USA Today. Available at: https://www.usatoday.com/story/money/personalfinance/2024/04/02/retirement-magic-number-study/73170172007/ (Accessed: 05 November 2024).

◇ Mike Winters (2024) How much money you need to retire comfortably in every U.S. state, CNBC. Available at: https://www.cnbc.com/2024/10/02/how-much-money-you-need-to-retire-comfortably-in-every-us-state.html (Accessed: 05 November 2024).

◇ Millions of older Americans are nearing retirement without a penny in savings, CBS News. Available at: https://www.cbsnews.com/news/retirement-baby-boomers-with-no-retirement-savings/ (Accessed: 05 November 2024).

◇ Suknanan, J. (2023) Here's how much money 25-year-olds need to invest every month to become a millionaire, CNBC. Available at: https://www.cnbc.com/select/how-much-25-year-olds-should-invest-monthly-to-become-a-millionaire/ (Accessed: 05 November 2024).

www.ingramcontent.com/pod-product-compliance
Lightning Source LLC
Chambersburg PA
CBHW030528210326
41597CB00013B/1062